MAKING FAIRIES

FAIRIES

&

FANTASTICAL CREATURES

How to Weave and Carve in Wool and Chenille

MAKING
FAIRIES
&
FANTASTICAL
CREATURES

How to Weave and Carve
in Wool and Chenille

Julie Sharp

Guild of Master Craftsman Publications Ltd

To my parents for a wonderfully interesting childhood – my father for
his creative influence and his humanity, and my mother for encouraging
my passion for fairies; to Alistair for his contribution and support;
to my boys James and Olly for their inspiration;
to my aunts Jillie and Hilary for their love and for influencing
my conscience for the planet; and finally to Mike, Pat, Bob, Chris, Lee,
Edie and Paul for their encouragement.

First published 2000 by
Guild of Master Craftsman Publications Ltd,
166 High Street, Lewes,
East Sussex, BN7 1XU

ISBN 1 86108 177 4

Illustrations by Julie Sharp
Cover photography by Chris Skarbon
Other photography by Chris Skarbon and Anthony Bailey
Author photograph by Patricia Graham
Designed by Phil and Traci Morash, Fineline Studios

Typeface: Phaistos Roman

Colour origination by Viscan Graphics (Singapore)
Printed and bound by Kyodo Printing (Singapore) under the supervision of MRM Graphics,
Winslow, Buckinghamshire, UK

Contents

Wonder where?

Ever wonder where fairies go?
From land to sea and dells they flow
Brightly, sprightly across the air
Flipping through tall grass with flair
Happy always wings so neat
Touching softly with tiny kissing feet
Air gusts in with just a trace
Sifting through tall brush with grace
Look to see to catch them somewhere
The place they'll be could be just under there
Hope to find one on my nose
Too fast for me when I wake from a doze
You'll know somehow a fairy's been
Feels like magic has cast and splashed its gleam

Julie Sharp

Introduction

As a child I loved to create toys from lots of different found items. I liked to make little things that fit easily into a pocket – tiny little dolls made from thread and dustbin-bag ties, and little people with hats made from pencil erasers and drawing pins. I was always creating things from my imagination by using materials that were simple, affordable and readily available. I enjoyed the challenge of making things that could not be bought in a shop.

A few years back I was in the States, and stopped at a store where I discovered an interesting selection of pipe cleaners, sold in what looked like packages left over from the sixties. On a whim, I bought lots of colours and left, my brain bubbling with ideas. That's how all this began.

For me, the joy of play comes from the process of creating something new from my imagination, and from learning to see things differently. The challenge of problem-solving and getting to the next level brings its own rewards. With play, the creative landscape is endless. The motivation for producing this book is to inspire you to create your own characters and landscapes, and to satisfy your creative impulses.

The projects I have designed make use of inexpensive materials and equipment, and are geared to all levels of experience and ability. If you can unpick wool from an old sweater and thread a needle, you have the skills you need to make these projects.

The materials and tools required can fit into a little portable container. You can make the projects on your knee, in front of the television, while chatting with friends, waiting at a bus stop, sitting on a train, and so on. Making fairies is a fun way to pass the time.

Once complete, some of the projects have delicate parts. The chenille stems, or pipe cleaners, have a metal wire core and can bend. If crushed by a small hand, they may need adjusting back into their original form. Consider the delicacy required to handle a real live fairy; you wouldn't just put her down anywhere...

The projects are vehicles for skill-building and creative development. To help you gauge the complexity of each project, I have graded them 0–5, with 0 being the easiest and 5 the most difficult. You will notice at the beginning of each project a flower motif with five petals. The pink-coloured petals signal the grade of the project.

Once you get going on the projects and gain confidence, with simple adjustments like changing the wool or adding a set of wings to a character, you can expand on the designs. Before you know it, you will be able to create a world of unique characters. Have lots of fun!

Equipment and Materials

Equipment

All items included here are widely available and reasonably inexpensive to buy.

Pompom discs

You will need three sizes for these projects: large (5.5cm (2⅛in) in diameter); medium (3.5cm (1⅜in) in diameter); small (2cm (¾in) in diameter). Using one side of the pompom disc only gives you a slightly smaller pompom for that disc size. To create handmade discs made from cut-out cardboard, refer to the pompom disc templates in Techniques (page 9).

Sewing and craft needles

Have a range of sizes to hand, from the fine beading needles to those which accommodate a dense strand of wool.

Needle-nose pliers or tweezers

You will find these invaluable for manipulating pipe cleaners and chenille stems.

A pair of embroidery or small sharp scissors

These are very useful for a whole range of tasks. A good, small pair of sharp scissors is really a priority for this work. Try and buy the best pair available and keep them well-maintained.

Utility scissors or wire cutters

These are very effective for snapping the wire in chenille stems and pipe cleaners.

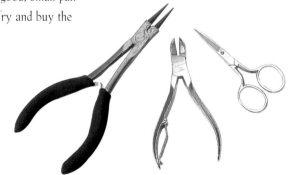

Battery-operated shaver (optional)

To give the surface of the handmade pompoms a smooth finish in the final refining stage of the projects.

Ruler

Use a transparent ruler if possible. It is very useful when measuring parts of your models to match arms and legs.

Materials

Tip The measurements given for materials are in both metric and imperial systems, although I tend to favour metric. They have been rounded up or down to the nearest millimetre or convenient equivalent. As you work, use either metric or imperial measurements; do not mix units.

You need few basic materials to complete these projects even old knitted jumpers will do!

Wool

Wool is available in many brands and in different shades, textures and yarn content. I do not use a particular brand for these projects. Your main considerations when selecting wool are the colour, thickness and finish of the thread, and whether it is made of natural or synthetic fibres. Chunky wools are unsuitable because of the delicate nature of the projects featured in this book; thick gauge, for example, is not appropriate. As a guide, do not use threads thicker than the Aran variety. Angora is suitable in terms of thread thickness, but takes a little longer to wind around pompom discs than other wools. For some of the projects, wool with a high cotton content is best. Cotton has less give, so when you pull on the thread it does not stretch as far as other threads. This is an advantage when making smaller pompoms. Have a range of wools to create the handmade pompoms, including multicoloured and metallic yarns.

Pompoms

Pompoms are used for the main structure of the fairies and creatures, and other parts, for example the tail, head, face, nose, neck and any sections that need to be thicker than the chenille stems available to you.

Handmade pompoms

Make the main body parts of the models with handmade pompoms. For these you will need to use the pompom discs listed in Equipment (page 2). The pompoms can be trimmed, carved and sewn together to create almost any shape. Additional thread or three-dimensional weaving can be sewn into the fabric of the pompoms to create lumps and bumps, to increase their density and thereby emphasize the shape and character of the models. Add sparkle to your handmade pompoms by interweaving a bit of glittery or metallic embroidery thread.

Commercially made pompoms

These are available in a range of sizes and colours, including glittery varieties and are great fun to use.

Although small pompoms can be handmade with difficulty, it is almost impossible to make them delicate enough for some of the tiniest fairy parts, like the eyes, nose, neck, buttons and other accent pieces. In any case, enough effort is spent creating the main structural pompoms. It is easier to purchase them. If the tiniest pompoms are not readily available, you can use craft felt or embroidery thread in place of these accent items.

Commercially made pompoms are sometimes sold loose, and are not labelled for size. Even those sold in packs and labelled as a specific size often have slight variations in size within the same batch. In the projects that follow therefore, the sizes given should be regarded as approximate. When selecting specific pompoms, spread them out on your work surface and assess which are most appropriate for the task.

Chenille stems or pipe cleaners

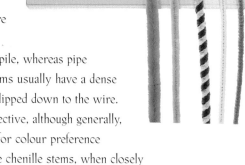

Available in a range of colours, sizes, textures and pile densities. Choose stems in interesting colours and patterns – the more varied your range, the more possibilities you have for creative ideas.

Chenille stems usually have a synthetic acrylic pile, whereas pipe cleaners usually have a cotton fabric pile. Cotton stems usually have a dense pile and are better suited for pieces that need to be clipped down to the wire. Clipping the pile away on synthetic stems is also effective, although generally, these are more favourable than cotton pipe cleaners for colour preference rather than pile density and texture. Compared to the chenille stems, when closely clipped, the cotton stems tend to give a neater finish, and the pile remaining on the wire has better coverage. Cotton stems, however, seem to be available in a more limited range of colours, textures and sizes.

Tip Parental guidance is advised for young children when using pipe cleaners. To protect small hands against sharp points, fold over the ends when not in use.

Individually, stems are used to create arms, legs and antennae, flower petals and leaves, and can be trimmed into different shapes for each. They can also be interlaced to create larger three-dimensional projects, for example the tree house, the bird's nest and the pink flowers. These are made by linking and looping the chenille stems with your hands or a pair of needle-nose pliers.

I created most of the legs for the fairies using the thicker synthetic stems. The pile needs to be thicker to give you room to define leg, calf and knee shapes. In each project, I give specific measurements for the thickness of stems required for the arms and legs. If you choose stems slightly thicker than suggested, you will have more latitude to develop the surface character of the model.

Sewing and embroidery thread

These are available in a range of colours and finishes.

Craft felt

This is available in a range of colours, and is very useful for making clothes and accessories.

Transparent or opaque plastic

These sheets of plastic are rigid and often slightly opaque, and can be cut out from folders available from stationery suppliers. It is also available as packaging.

Techniques

There are just a few basic techniques required to make your projects, from thinking through your designs to making pompoms, sculpting limbs, sewing clothes and cutting out wings for your fairies. Once you have completed a few projects, you will gain the confidence to expand on the designs in this book and create your own unique fairy and creature characters.

There are four basic steps to consider when thinking about creating your fairy or creature project.

Selecting your materials

Select the correct sizes and colours of stems and pompoms for your project. The materials you select establish the character of the model and are key to its final appearance.

Using stems and pipe cleaners

Always buy the straightest pipe cleaners available. The wire has a bit of a memory, and if you require a straight stem, it is difficult to straighten it out again after it has had

a curl or bend put in it. The best way to manipulate pipe cleaners and chenille stems, for example when making antennae for the fairies, is to use a pair of needle-nose pliers or tweezers.

To make angles in your stems, use the corner of an object against which to shape the stem. If you want to make a curl in your stem, bend it around a pen or pencil, use your pliers, or simply pull the stem between thumb and finger from one end of the stem.

To create a coil, again manipulate the stem around a pencil or a pen into a twist. The size of the curls in the coil will be determined by the circumference of the pencil, or other object that you use.

Different techniques for looping and coiling the stems

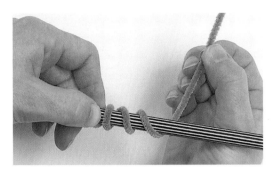

Curling a stem with a pen

Using the pliers to manipulate folds and bends

To break the length of a pipe cleaner without using a cutting tool, bend it repeatedly in the same spot, and the wire will eventually snap. If you have a good pair of utility scissors or wire cutters, use them to snap through the wire of a pipe cleaner or chenille stem.

Trimming and moulding to create contours

To define the contours of a character's parts from the stems and pompoms, you need to trim and sculpt. A small, sharp pair of scissors really helps with this procedure, as parts of the models are quite small and intricate.

Three-dimensional weaving and sewing

Trimming a stem into shape

Three-dimensional weaving is used to build up the structure of the individual handmade pompoms on a variety of projects, for example the toadstool or berry, and to connect a series of pompoms together to create characters like Pink worm and Dragonfly fairy. This technique strengthens and defines the shape of the pompoms, and is sometimes key to achieving the character of the model. You can embellish the detail as much as you like.

To weave three-dimensionally involves weaving the thread across the pompom body from

Refining the model with a sharp pair of scissors

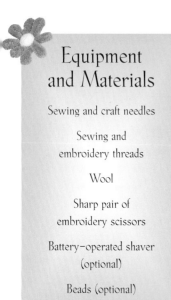

Equipment and Materials

Sewing and craft needles

Sewing and embroidery threads

Wool

Sharp pair of embroidery scissors

Battery-operated shaver (optional)

Beads (optional)

Weaving wool three-dimensionally to build up the structure

side to side in a cross-like fashion. The more threads woven into the structure of the pompom, the more dense the model becomes. As you work, an internal web of fibres develops until filled to capacity, creating a completely solid shape, and it becomes increasingly difficult to insert the needle and wool thread into the surface of the pompom model. At this stage, you can choose to use a battery-operated shaver or sharp scissors to shape, carve and smooth the pompom, which improves the overall appearance of the final piece. To bring variety to your design, you can add woven spots of colour to specific areas of the model.

In their rough, untrimmed state, the pompoms have a soft quality, and sometimes you may wish to leave them like this to achieve a desired effect. Matte Moth fairy was largely made with raw, unshaped pompoms which add a certain quality to the character. Keep this in mind when creating your own projects.

Not all of the projects require a three-dimensional weaving feature in their technique. If you need to attach two or more handmade pompoms together with sewing thread, improve the quality and strength of the connections between them by adding extra thread through the joined centres. When attaching commercially made pompoms, follow the same procedure, but use finer sewing thread instead. Commercially made pompoms are less stable and manipulable than the handmade variety, and they cannot be woven three-dimensionally with additional thread to build up a specific surface area.

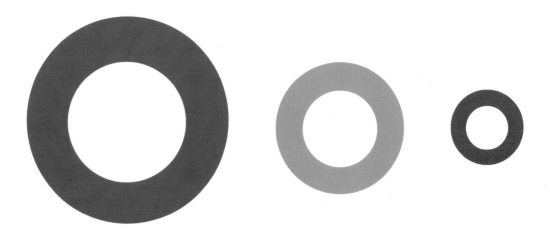

Pompoms

How to make pompom disc templates

The pompom discs used to make the projects in this book were purchased from a craft shop. They are made of hard plastic, and two discs are supplied to form a disc ring to make each pompom.

You do not have to buy your pompom discs, however; they can be handmade, too. They will not be as durable as the commercially made discs, but the advantage of making your own is that you can adjust the dimensions to create various different-sized pompoms. If you do make your own, use a piece of cardboard which can easily be cut with your scissors; perhaps card from a cereal box, or recycled stiff-backed envelopes.

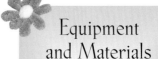

Equipment and Materials

Pieces of cardboard

Sharp pair of scissors

Pencil

Pair of compasses

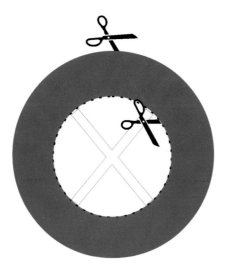

The projects featured in this book use three disc sizes only: 5.5cm (2⅛in) in diameter, 3.5cm (1⅜in) in diameter and 2cm (¾in) in diameter. All of the models that require handmade pompoms were created using these dimensions.

Equipment and Materials

Two same-size cardboard discs

Wool

Sharp pair of scissors

Craft needle (large enough to thread wool)

1 Select the most rigid card that you can cut through with a pair of craft scissors, and marking the inner and outer dimensions, draw the disc shape onto it. If it is helpful, use a pair of compasses.

2 Cut around the circumference of your shape, then a hole in the centre of the disc to the dimension of the inner circle. Remove the card circle from the middle.

3 Make a second identical disc.

Tip   The inner circles will not have an especially smooth edge when hand-cut with a pair of craft scissors, but this will not affect the shape of the pompom in any way.

How to make pompoms by hand

1 Place the two discs together to form a disc ring. Double-thread the needle with wool to speed the application. Tie a knot once over through the central hole of the discs to secure them together, before winding the thread of wool around the disc.

2 When necessary, re-thread your needle and simply tuck through an existing layer of thread onto the surface of the discs and continue to apply another layer of wool.

3 Pull the thread tightly as the layers build up. When it is no longer possible to fit the needle through the centre hole of the disc ring, the pompom thread is ready to be cut and the discs separated.

4 Place a small, sharp pair of scissors into the wool on the outside edge of the filled disc ring. Cut all the way around, severing all the thread loops from the centre of the disc ring.

5 Trim around the outside edges to tidy away loose strands of thread, allowing room for a length of wool thread to be tied around the centre of the grouped threads.

6 Tie a knot as tightly as possible; this holds everything together. To reinforce it, it is a good idea to tie a second thread, too. This is what I call the central thread. When you later reinforce the pompom with a web of woven threads, this central thread becomes less vital in holding the pompom together. Pull the rings slightly apart to expose the strands in-between the two discs.

7 The pompom is now ready for trimming, carving and sculpting.

Tip   To create the neatest, thickest pompoms, wind the wool firmly and evenly around the pompom discs, one layer at a time. This adds to the overall density of the pompom, creating a fuller effect.

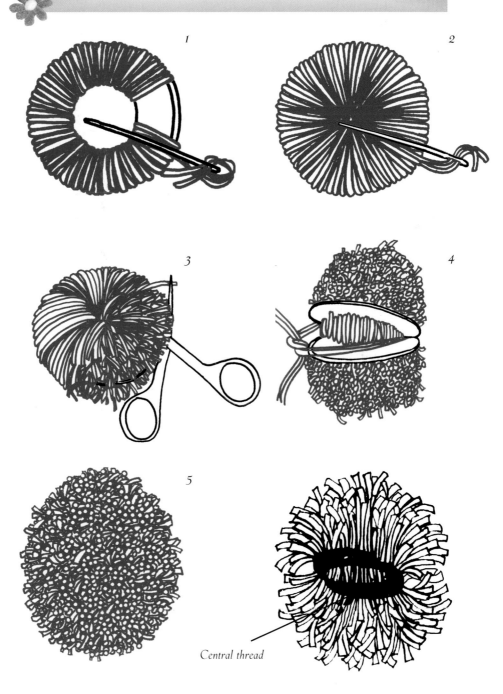

1

2

3

4

5

Central thread

Half-and-half pompoms

A half-and-half-colour pompom is achieved by simply applying the threads to the disc ring into two distinct sections.

1 Wind wool in the first colour around one section. Build up the layers of wool in this colour until you have filled one half of the discs.
2 Fill the remaining half of the disc ring by layering the second colour until it is full.

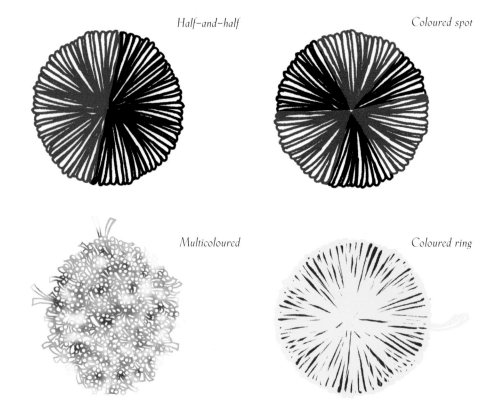

Half-and-half

Coloured spot

Multicoloured

Coloured ring

Pompoms with coloured spots

To create different-coloured spots in your pompom, apply layers of colour in pie-shaped segments.

1 Build up the mass of wool threads, keeping the same-coloured thread in each pie-shaped segment.
2 Alternate the above with thinner bands of colour to create small spots on the completed pompom.

Coloured ring pompoms

1 To create a colour ring, apply a full layer or two of wool around the entire circumference of the disc ring.

2 Take a different-coloured wool thread and apply a layer or two, covering the first layers completely.

3 Take the original wool thread and apply it a second time, covering the layers underneath and the full diameter of the disc ring. Fill with this thread until full.

4 When the pompom thread is removed from the disc and the central thread is secured, you will see a coloured ring in the middle of the pompom shape.

Multicoloured pompoms

Create these with multicoloured wool. To enhance the effect, when threading the pompom with additional wool, cluster groups of the same colour by threading through to an area of a similar colour. For a glittery pompom, use metallic thread instead.

Joining pompoms

Smaller pompoms can be joined using fine sewing thread or silk. It is unnecessary to absolutely match the thread to the colour of your pompoms because the pile usually covers the thread. However it is useful to have a range of different-coloured threads as the smallest pompoms will not hide the thread quite as well.

Join handmade pompoms with the same pompom thread unless indicated otherwise to avoid flecks of different-coloured thread appearing on the surface of the pompom.

Reducing and enlarging the projects

Projects such as Pink worm, Grasshopper, Daisy fairy and Matte Moth fairy can be adjusted to whatever size you desire by making or buying pompoms in different dimensions to fit.

To adjust the sizes and keep the model in proportion too, simply photocopy the template to a reduced or enlarged size. Use a ruler to measure the sizes from the reduced or enlarged copy to maintain the proportion and character of the project.

> Tip   You may be tempted to use glue to join items, but glue is not very flexible when you want to reposition something or change your mind. Also, if the glue seal breaks, it is not forgiving and can destroy or mark the surface. I recommend that you use needle and sewing thread to join the models together, which means that if a section needs repositioning it is a simple process to adjust it.

Clothes and accessories

Fairy clothes

Each garment pattern is designed to involve very little sewing. The fabric best suited for these garments is craft felt; it is soft, easily manipulable and does not unravel which means that it is not necessary to hem the edges.

Once a pattern is cut from the felt it needs only a few stitches to sew it together. The circular skirt pieces can be fitted onto the characters without any sewing. The garments are interchangeable, creating a larger range of outfits. You can extend the variety of available options by changing the colour of the felt, adding beads and ribbons, or by using pinking shears to serrate the edge of the fabric. You can also decorate the fairy outfits with items such as lace, embroidery thread and fabric paint. Some of the characters' wings may be too large to fit into some of the garment pieces so these outfits are more ideally suited to the characters with smaller wings. You can adapt any of the patterns to accommodate those fairies with larger wings.

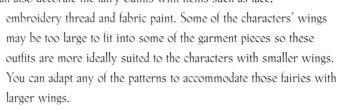

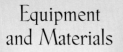

Equipment and Materials

Sharp pair of scissors

Sewing and craft needles

Sewing threads

Craft felt
(various colours)

Decorative accessories,
e.g. lace, beads, ribbon
(optional)

A selection of 5mm (¼in)
commercially made pompoms
(to make buttons)

1 Select one of the patterns.
2 To create a template, take a piece of paper or plastic and trace the pattern onto it. Place this template over a piece of felt and cut out the garment.
3 To join the edges of a garment together, pinch each side together to form a dart where the 'x' marks appear on the template, and sew into position.
4 To make a button, take a 5mm (¼in) commercially made pompom and sew into place. Adjust the position to fit the individual fairy.
5 To make a buttonhole, find the appropriate position on the garment, and cut a tiny slit to create an opening for the little pompom button to pop through.
6 To make slits in the skirts, follow the perforated lines on the templates.

Dress

Flower

Leaf

Wrist and ankle flowers

Front straps of
pinafore dress

Pompom button

Pinafore dress

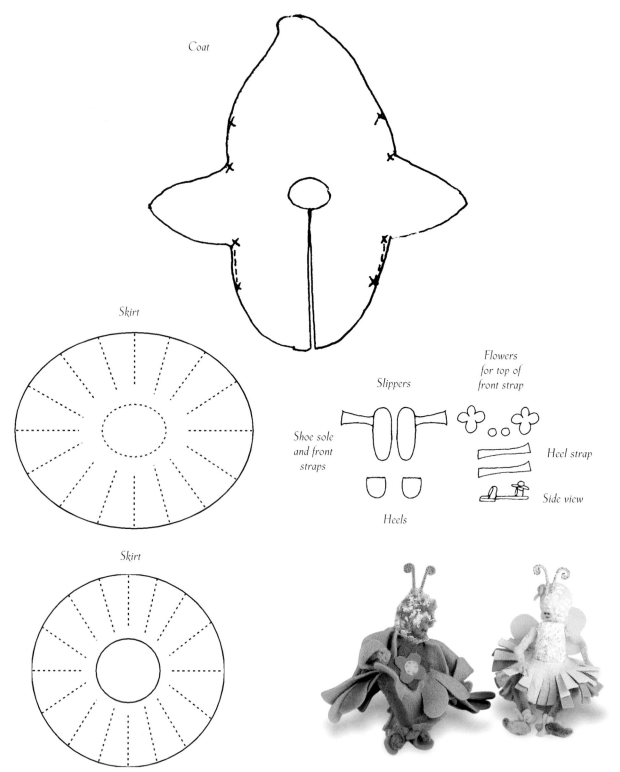

Coat

Skirt

Slippers

Flowers
for top of
front strap

Shoe sole
and front
straps

Heel strap

Side view

Heels

Skirt

Fairy slippers

Prettify your fairy with these colour co-ordinated little slippers.

1 First take your craft felt and cut out the shapes from the templates.

2 Fold the strap over on the slipper and sew into position.

3 Position the cut-out felt flower onto the middle of the strap, and a 3mm (⅛in) pompom on top of that, then sew together. To modify this design, you can make a leaf shape rather than a flower and to do this, remove two of the flower petals.

4 Place the cut-out felt heel at the opposite end from the strap.

5 Optionally, attach a second strap to the top side of the slipper, aligning it with the inner edge of the heel. Delicately sew either side of the strap to the base of the slipper.

Fairy wings

Make these delightful wings from opaque plastic folders or packaging materials.

1 Select a sheet of plastic. It must be sturdy enough not to crease when handled, but flexible enough so that a pair of utility scissors can cut through it. For some of the more fiddly angles and curves, use a small sharp pair of scissors. Cut a square large enough to fit the entire wing span of each pattern.

2 To create the wing pattern, place a traced outline of the wing shape onto the cut-out plastic rectangle. Fold the sheet in half down the middle to create a seam. Place the traced outline of the wing shape, also folded in half, overtop of the seam as a guide.

3 Cut through the plastic around the outside edge of the wing pattern, following the shape.

4 Use the centre fold as the contact point for sewing the wings onto the fairies.

5 Take a thick craft needle and perforate the wing shape at the top and bottom of the centre of the fold. Pierce two holes next to each other just wide enough apart to thread a discreet stitch, so that the wool thread can pass through both and secure the wings onto the back of the fairy body. For larger fairies, make two sets of these holes, one above the other, before securing to the back of your fairy. The shape and character of the model will determine the location of the perforations.

6 Using the same thread as you did to sew the body, attach the wings. They will have a visible stitch on the seam of the wing which will blend into the background.

7 There are two wing pattern shapes with two separate pieces that make up the whole wing for the Lily fairy and Berry fairy. Overlap these sections slightly when securing them to the back of the fairies.

Equipment and Materials

Utility scissors

Sharp pair of scissors

Square of transparent or opaque plastic

Paper and pencil (for tracing)

Thick craft needle

Sewing thread

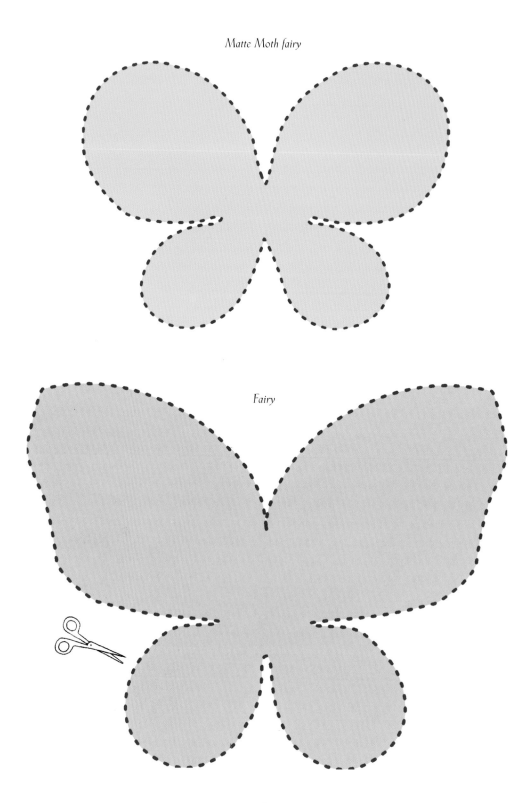

Matte Moth fairy

Fairy

Lily fairy

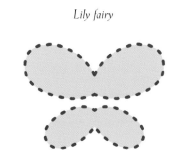

Honey Bea

Berry fairy

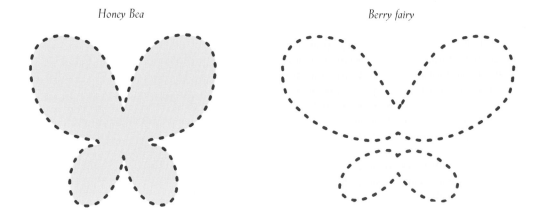

Dragonfly fairy

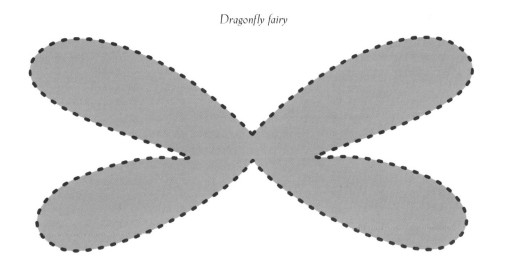

Making the fairies

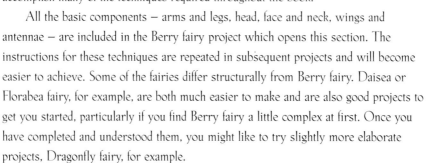

Once you have grasped the techniques for weaving, looping and coiling stems, most of the projects can be worked individually without having to complete them in sequence. With some variation in complexity, there is a basic method to making the fairies, and Berry fairy represents the best example of how to make a mid-level fairy. There are easier and more difficult fairies to make, but by making Berry fairy first you will accomplish many of the techniques required throughout the book.

All the basic components – arms and legs, head, face and neck, wings and antennae – are included in the Berry fairy project which opens this section. The instructions for these techniques are repeated in subsequent projects and will become easier to achieve. Some of the fairies differ structurally from Berry fairy. Daisea or Florabea fairy, for example, are both much easier to make and are also good projects to get you started, particularly if you find Berry fairy a little complex at first. Once you have completed and understood them, you might like to try slightly more elaborate projects, Dragonfly fairy, for example.

The projects are formatted in the same way to make them clear and accessible. Each includes instructions on how to make the fairy; photographic and diagrammatic references so that you can check your progress, and a list of equipment and materials. Many projects also include an assembly map, which consists of overlapping drawings showing the individual components of the fairy, and provide a quick visual reference for how the projects are made. The best way to start your project is to have all the required equipment and materials assembled close to hand.

The character of each model is quite unique. Do not expect to reproduce an exact clone of the models featured in this book. You can expect to make a fairy which closely resembles them, but your own will vary slightly depending on the equipment and materials you use, and your own interpretation. Use the instructions as a guideline, as your projects will ultimately have your own creative stamp, and once you have mastered the techniques, you can adjust individual parts to make them thinner, longer smaller, whatever – or by using different colours and accessories, to create your own unique characters.

You are now ready to make your first fairy!

The Fairies

Tiny ice crystals and stamen blush
Smaller than curls on the oxen tusk
Brave and bold but light as can be
Fairy sweet come home to me

Berry fairy

Berry fairy is a jaunty character with her multicoloured body, glittery antennae and flowery, bright green trim. She is the ideal medium-level project for testing out your new skills.

Legs

1 To make the legs, select a straight 17cm (6¾in) long chenille stem. Bend the stem in the middle around a circular object like a pen or pencil, about 1cm (⅜in) in diameter.

2 The top of the legs will now form a curve (not a sharp bend). To start working the feet, bend a 90° angle about 2.5cm (1in) from the bottom of each end of the stem.

3 Begin to shape the feet by using a sharp pair of craft scissors to cut a wedge shape at the tip of each foot, removing the pile from the stem as you do so.

Tip As the first fairy project, I have increased the measurements for her limbs to allow you more latitude to coil and loop the stems, without distorting the model. As you become adept, you will be able to manipulate them more accurately, and can adjust the lengths as necessary.

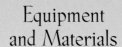

Equipment and Materials

Needle-nose pliers

Small, sharp pair of scissors

Wire cutters or utility scissors

Permanent marker pens

Felt-tip pen (pink)

Pompom discs: medium, 3.5cm (1⅜in) in diameter, and small, 2cm (¾in) in diameter

50g ball of wool (berry red)

50g ball of wool (multicoloured)

Wool gauge needle

Sewing needle and sewing thread (flesh-coloured)

1 chenille stem, 10cm x 7mm (4in x ¼in) (flesh-coloured)

1 chenille stem, 17cm x 1cm (6¾in x ⅜in) (sage green)

1 chenille stem, 7cm (2¾in) (glittery gold)

1 commercially made pompom, 1cm (⅜in) in diameter (flesh-coloured)

2 commercially made pompoms, 5mm (¼in) in diameter (flesh-coloured)

1 sheet of 8cm (3¼in) square transparent plastic

Craft felt, 10cm (4in) square (pale green)

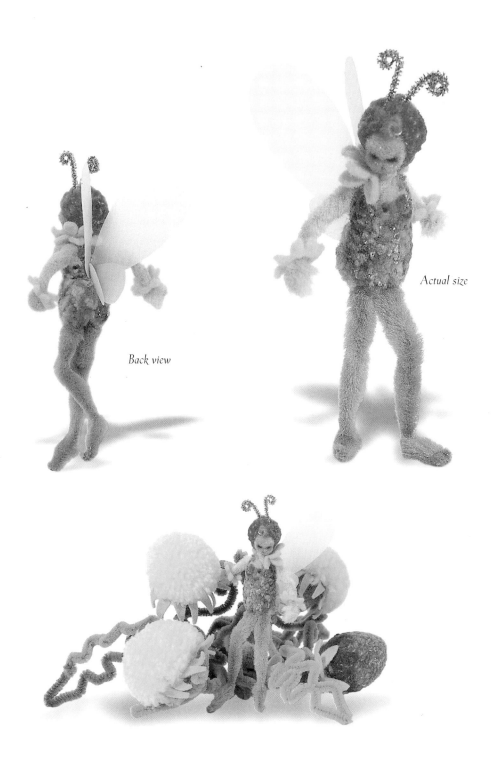

Actual size

Back view

4 With a pair of pliers, pinch the end of the wire
   and twist it around to create a curly-toe shape
   at the end of the foot. The sharp ends of the
   stem are now made safe, and the curls will
   create the impression that the fairy is sporting a pair of shoes.
   The foot should measure about 2cm (¾in) in length.

5 To create the ankles, trim indentations into the sides of the stem
   just above the foot bend.

6 Shape the sole of the foot by trimming a small indent in the
   underside. Leave a little pile at the heel of the foot.

7 Trim the shin into shape, leaving the front side flatter than the
   back of the calf.

8 Trim an indentation about 2.5cm (1in) up the stem from the heel,
   to create a curve in the back of the knee. Bend it back to pose the
   fairy's legs.

9 The legs are now ready to be attached to the body. You do not
   need to separate the legs into two because as a one-piece
   section woven into the body, it gives extra support to the model.
   Other parts can be connected together with the leg loop as well,
   a tail or bee sting for example.

Arms

1 To begin the arms, select a medium 10cm (4in) long flesh-
   coloured chenille stem for both arms.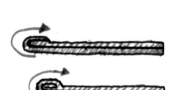

2 Using the needle-nose pliers, curl over one end of each arm by
   about 0.5cm (¼in) to create the hand shape.

3 The curled hand covers the sharp ends of the chenille stem. Make
   sure that both hands are the same size. Adjust the length of the
   arms at the shoulder when you create the arm loops.

4 To create the wrists, trim two indents on either side of the stem
   just above the hands. Shape the hands with a pair of sharp
   scissors, but be careful not to snip off too much of the pile.

5 Use the needle-nose pliers to create a loop at the tip of the shoulder end of the arms. Make sure that the loops tuck in under the arm and not outwards.

6 Using the sharp scissors, shape the remaining section of the arm, tapering inwards slightly at the elbow on the inner side. Create an indent on the inside of the arm about 2cm (¾in) up from the hand. Leave a point for the elbow on the outside of the arm.

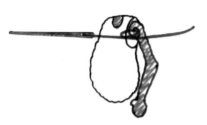

7 Now the arm can be attached to the body. Using a needle, pass a wool or sewing thread through the loops to attach the arm to the pompom body.

Tip When the component pieces are ready to assemble, the stems that form the arms and legs can bend out of shape, and should be handled with consideration.

Body

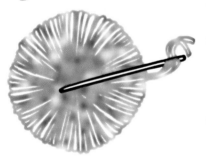

1 Make the pompom body with a medium-sized pompom disc and the multicoloured wool (see Techniques, page 10). Pack the pompom disc as full as possible with the thread.

2 Find the position of the central thread where it holds together the mass of wool threads, making sure it is horizontal as you work. This means that when you weave additional thread into the pompom to fill it out, the needle can pass through the middle of the pompom without obstruction. Depending on the project, it may not be necessary to keep an eye on the location of the central thread, but it helps to avoid cutting into it when clipping and shaping the pompom body.

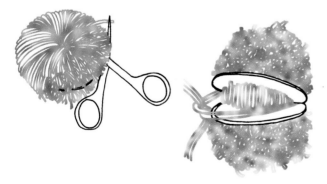

3 Keeping the thread level, establish the top and bottom of the pompom. These sections will be less dense than the centre of the pompom because the threads splay apart at the ends. This means that there is some flexibility when you need to attach legs and other parts, and when fitting other pompoms into the pile.

4 Begin to shape the fairy. To create a waistline, using a pair of sharp scissors, carve out large indentations by removing some of the material from the sides of the body pompom.

5 Continue to trim around the pompom, keeping in mind that you need to allow enough bulk to remain for the bottom, tummy and chest areas.

6 Once the sides are established, begin to trim away pile to round out the shoulders. It is best to trim the shoulders first because they are narrower than the bottom section of the fairy. Work around gradually, removing only a little pile at a time.

7 Define the chest, tummy and bottom sections with more woven thread, trimming as necessary. The overall shape should now be established.

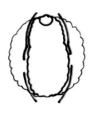

Tip A 50g ball of wool will be more than enough for use on each of the pompoms in this project, but is sold as a standard size. The extra wool will be handy for other pompom projects.

8 Position the loop at the top of the legs into the bottom centre of the pompom; it should slip in quite easily at this stage. It becomes more difficult to position the leg loop as the structure of the body is built up with additional woven thread. Sew the legs to the body with wool thread.

9 Fill out, smooth and finish any areas that need thickening and refining. Problem areas are the top and bottom of the pompom. Target the desired area, and pass the threaded needle through the entire body area, clipping off threads to the desired length, and gradually building up the structure until complete. You can also do this if you want to add in spots of colour to a differently shaded section.

10 To create the 'swim suit' look of the fairy's body, you need first to create the armpit. Sew flesh-coloured thread through the top of the body to create a cluster of threads on each side of the upper torso where the armpit is located. Fit the arm loops into these circular flesh-coloured areas; these should be large enough to overlap the placement of the arm loop. This is an optional detail.

11 You can also apply flesh-coloured wool to the neck area of the body pompom where the neck pompom fits. Enter the needle through the armpit section, and weave up through the top of the neck. Trim the thread off at the neck. If you thread the needle with a double thickness of thread, it will make this process more precise and save a little time.

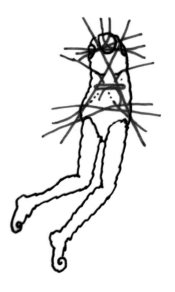

12 Once you have completed this effect, finish off by joining the pompom neck and head to the top of the pompom body by sewing on with finer sewing thread than the wool. Pass the needle and thread through the body a few times to make sure that the head is firmly attached.

Head

1　To create Berry fairy's head, make a small pompom using the 2cm (¾in) pompom discs and the berry red wool. Use one half of the discs only to make a less dense pompom than for the body.

2　To shape the head, start clipping away pile from each side of the pompom. As you work, keep in mind that you are trying to achieve an acorn shape.

3　The head measures just less than 2cm (¾in) in diameter. It is a bit tricky to achieve this so be careful not to cut into the central thread or it may unravel. Some of the fairies have additional threads woven through their hair, forming a knobbly texture, but Berry fairy wears only a curl at the top of her forehead. To achieve this, use the berry-coloured wool thread to weave a bobble of threads and secure into place.

4　To join the head and face, position a 1cm (⅜in) commercially made flesh-coloured pompom, representing the face, into the pile of the pompom head. Push the fibres to the sides of the face pompom to embed it into the pile. The face should be inserted at the bottom of the pompom head to emphasize the hairline above the forehead which enhances the acorn shape.

5　Sew the two pompoms together with needle and thread.

6　To create the contours for the eyes, carve an indentation into the flesh-coloured pompom. Using a black and a red permanent ink pen, dot two black eyes and one red mouth onto the surface of the pompom face. This process can be applied before or after attaching the head and the face.

7 To create the neck, attach two small flesh-coloured commercially made pompoms, one on top of the other, below the pompom face.

8 An alternative method for making a neck is to select a small length of flesh-coloured chenille stem, about 1.5cm (⅝in) long. Loop at either end with a pair of needle-nose pliers or tweezers. Attach one side of this length of stem from the base of the head to the top of the torso, and the other side to the pompom head.

Antennae

1 To create the antennae, select a chenille stem about 7cm (2¾in) long. The antennae tend to catch on clothes, like wool sweaters, so do be careful. Differences in colour, texture, density and quality between types of pipe cleaner and chenille stem will have an effect on the final appearance of the antennae. I find that the best materials for the antennae are cotton stems or pipe cleaners.

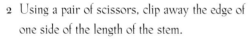

2 Using a pair of scissors, clip away the edge of one side of the length of the stem.

3 Remove the pile almost down to the wire from one side. Remove the remaining pile from the other sides of the stem, too. You should be left with a thin, velvety wire.

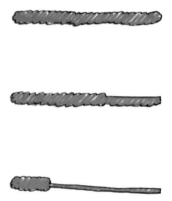

4 To create a big curl at either end of the antennae, take the needle-nose pliers and keep wrapping the very end of the thin end of the stem around the outside of the pliers until you achieve a full curl. The thin stem enables the curl to be more visible.

5 Repeat this process to the other end of the stem, but rotate consistently so that each side is balanced. The more rotations you make, the more dense the curl. Fold the stem in the middle to make a V shape.

6 Position the antennae gently into the pile of the fairy head. If you like, play with its position before sewing in, as this can alter the appearance of the character. Sew the antennae on by winding and tying a knot across the fold. Sew through the head and neck, passing the thread through both to secure the whole section.

Wings

1 Berry fairy has a fairly tall set of wings, but you can choose one of the other wing shapes if you wish. Using the pattern and following the instructions (see Techniques, page 19), make the Berry fairy wings.

2 Use the same multicoloured thread and a craft needle to attach the wings to the back of the fairy.

Finishing touches

1 For the finishing touch, make the hand and ankle decorations from a piece of craft felt in pale green to match the legs. For the neck flower, take a 3cm (1¼in) square section of felt and cut out the large flower. Fold it in half and attach to the back of Berry fairy's neck. Sew it into the fabric of the pompom body.

2 Use a 2cm (¾in) square piece of fabric for the smaller ankle and wrist flowers; they do not require any sewing and can be slipped onto the fairy. Following the pattern, left, cut a similar shape from the felt fabric. Cut one large flower for a collar and four smaller flowers for the wrists and ankles.

3 To add a blush to Berry fairy's cheeks, use a pink water–based felt tip and delicately rub the pen over the cheek area.

Neck and ankle and wrist flowers

Assembly map

The assembly map (above, right) illustrates all the components and stages required to make the delightful Berry fairy.

Daisea fairy

Daisea is the easiest and most adorable of the fairies to make. The project requires a little sewing to attach the individual parts together. If you want to give your fairy a pair of antennae, you will need needle-nose pliers to twist the ends into a curl, and your selected chenille stems will require some trimming.

Legs

1 To begin the Daisea fairy, collect together fourteen of the 5mm (¼in) flesh-coloured pompoms. Using a needle and thread, puncture through the centre of two sets of four pompoms and string them together to create the leg sections.

2 To make the fairy's shoes, take the 1cm (⅜in) in diameter peach or pink pompoms and clip away one edge of each to create a flat surface for the soles. Do not trim too much away or you may cut the central thread in the pompom and unravel it. Attach these two pompoms to each separate leg, positioning the flat side on the bottom.

Equipment and Materials

Sewing needle

Needle-nose pliers

Small pair of craft scissors

Permanent marker pen

1 chenille stem or pipe cleaner, 3cm (1¼in) (white)

1 commercially made pompom, 1cm (⅜in) in diameter (flesh-coloured)

14 commercially made pompoms, 5mm (¼in) in diameter (flesh-coloured)

1 commercially made pompom, 3mm (⅛in) in diameter (flesh-coloured)

1 commercially made pompom, 1.5cm (⅝in) in diameter (glittery, any colour)

2 commercially made pompoms, 1cm (⅜in) in diameter (peach or pink)

3 commercially made pompoms, 5mm (¼in) in diameter (glittery yellow)

1 commercially made pompom, 1.5cm (⅝in) in diameter (glittery yellow)

1 commercially made pompom, 2cm (¾in) in diameter (glittery yellow)

1 sheet of 3cm (1¼in) square transparent or opaque plastic

32

Daisea fairy

Front view

Actual size 70mm (2¾in) from the tip of the antennae to the heel

Arms

1 To make the arms, repeat the method you used for the legs. Take a needle and thread and string three 5mm (¼in) flesh-coloured pompoms together for each arm.

Body

1 Sew together the 2cm (1in) glittery yellow pompom for the fairy's bottom to the 1.5cm (⅝in) glittery yellow pompoms to form the chest and shoulders.

2 Attach the two 5mm (¼in) shoulder pompoms to either side of the chest pompom, near to the top of the pompom body.

3 To make the neck, position two 5mm (¼in) flesh-coloured pompoms together and sew into place on the top of the centre of the chest pompom.

4 Take the threaded pompom arms and, with needle and thread, secure each to just underneath the shoulder pompoms on both sides of the fairy.

5 Position the threaded pompom legs-and-feet to the pompom bottom. Space the legs about 5mm (¼in) apart, and sew them into the fabric of the pompom body.

6 Using a 5mm (¼in) yellow glittery pompom as a tail, position it onto the centre of the back of the fairy and attach with a needle and thread. The tail helps to give the fairy balance when she sits on her bottom.

Head

1 Sew the 1cm (⅜in) flesh-coloured pompom, representing the fairy's face, to the bottom of the 1.5cm (⅝in) pompom head.

2 Sew the tiny pompom nose in the centre of the pompom face.

Antennae

1 To make the antennae, take a white pipe cleaner and cut off a piece about 3cm (1¼in) in length. Trim the pile from all sides so that it barely covers the wire, and use the needle-nose pliers to twist the end of each stem into a tight curl.

2 Bend the stem in the middle and sew the antennae into the pile of the pompom head.

Wings

1 Now make Daisea's wings. Select the Lily fairy wings from the templates (see Techniques, page 19), but cut out the bottom smaller section only from the transparent or opaque plastic.

2 Sew the wings onto the fairy's pompom back.

Finishing touches

Take a permanent ink pen and dot two eyes just above and to each side of the nose.

Daisea assembly map

This assembly map illustrates all components and stages required to make your very own little Daisea fairy.

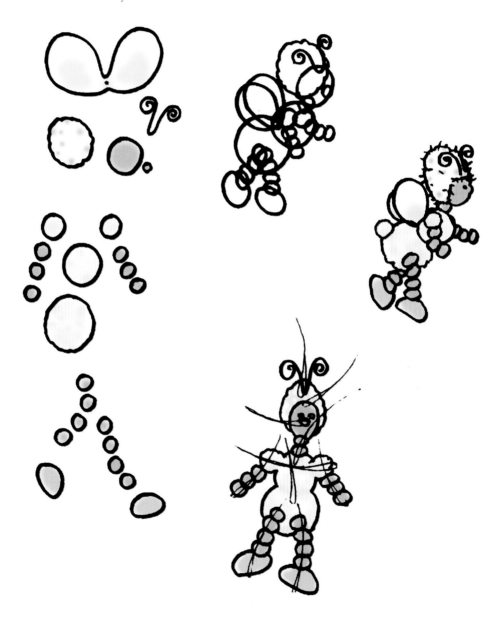

Florabea fairy

Like Daisea fairy, Florabea is a simple fairy to make and a good project to get you started, as she does not require any three-dimensional weaving. Maintaining the same proportion, Florabea can be made in a larger size using handmade pompoms. Almost all you need to do is trim off the ends of two commercially made pompoms and make a pair of arms and legs – it's as simple as that!

Legs

1 To begin this fairy, first make a pair of legs from a flesh-coloured cotton stem. Cut a 6.5cm (2⅝in) length to include both legs, each measuring about 2cm (¾in) long, and a bit in-between to attach to the fairy's lower body.

2 For the feet, take the chenille stem and bend 5mm (¼in) from one end to make a foot. Trim into a wedge shape. Repeat for the other foot.

3 Delicately shape the ankle of the foot, and repeat for the other one.

4 To make the knees, bend the stem legs about 1cm (⅜in) up from the bottom of the heel. Using the pair of sharp scissors, trim indentations on the inside of each knee bend.

5 Bend the pipe cleaner in the middle and cut into two to create the two legs.

6 Create a tiny loop about 1cm (⅜in) from the knee bends at the top thigh end of the stem. The loop will be used to anchor the leg into the pompom for the lower body.

7 To finish the legs, sew a 3mm (⅛in) pompom onto each foot to create slippers and to help

Equipment and Materials

Needle-nose pliers

Small pair of craft scissors

Sewing needle and thread (lavender)

1 chenille stem about 7cm (2¾in) in length (purple)

1 cotton chenille stem approximately 14cm (5½in) in length and 5mm (¼in) thick (flesh-coloured)

1 commercially made pompom 3mm (⅛in) in diameter (pale- or flesh-coloured)

1 commercially made pompom, 5mm (¼in) in diameter (flesh-coloured)

1 commercially made pompom 1cm (⅜in) in diameter (glittery)

2 commercially made pompoms, 5mm (¼in) in diameter (pale yellow or white)

2 commercially made pompoms 3mm (⅛in) in diameter (lilac)

3 pieces of lace in a flowery design, or alternatively, 3 small pieces of craft felt (white, cream or pink)

36

*Actual size 60mm (2⅜in)
from the tip of the
antennae to the heel*

Back view

soften the sharp ends of the stem feet. Select a colour that matches the pompom body. Set the legs aside for a moment until you are ready to assemble the whole fairy.

Arms

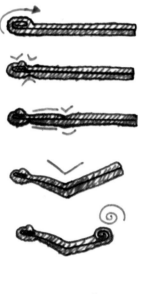

1 To create the arms, take a 2cm (¾in) length of the flesh-coloured pipe cleaner and, using the needle-nose pliers, fold over one end of each to create the hands.

2 To define the wrists, trim indentations at either side and just above the hands. Bend the hands inwards at the wrist.

3 To work the elbows, bend the arm about 1cm (⅜in) from the wrist. Trim small indentations into the inside of the arms.

4 Make loops at the top end of the arm stems so that they can be sewn into the upper body pompom with a needle and thread. The final arm length should be about 12mm (½in) in length. Set these aside for the moment.

Body

1 Take both the upper body pompom and the bottom pompom, and trim off the edges of each to create a flat surface where they join.

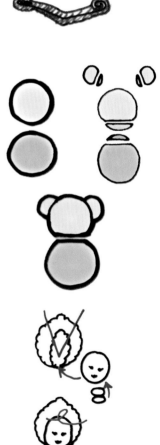

2 Take the two pompom shoulders, attach them to the top and sides of the upper torso pompom. Sew the upper and lower torso pompoms together. If you wish, add a piece of lace or craft felt between the two parts to create a decorative waistline before sewing them together.

3 Using the needle and lavender thread, attach the arms to the underside of each of the shoulder pompoms.

4 Spacing them nicely apart, sew the legs to the bottom of the lower body pompom.

Head

1 Attach the face and head together by embedding the 5mm (¼in) face pompom into the pile of the 1cm (⅜in) commercially made pompom head. Sew together using needle and thread.

2 For the neck, take the 3mm (⅛in) flesh- or pale-coloured pompom and assemble together with the head and body with needle and thread. If you wish, insert the two pieces of lace or craft felt between the head and shoulders. If you use the craft felt, first cut out flower shapes using the wrist and ankle patterns.

Antennae

1 Create a pair of antennae from a purple 5cm (¼in) long chenille stem. Clip away the pile almost down to the wire.

2 Bend it in the middle and create two curls at either end using the needle-nose pliers to pinch the stem ends. With a needle and thread, sew to the top of the pompom head.

Wings

Finally, make a pair of wings for Florabea fairy (see Techniques, page 19). Florabea's wings are composed of the small lower section of the template for Lily fairy's wings.

Florabea assembly map

This assembly map illustrates all components and stages required to make your own Florabea fairy.

Matte Moth Fairy

Matte Moth fairy is a very jolly and useful character, having two pairs of arms and a wonderful long tail, for which you need to make a few lavender blue handmade pompoms. Once complete, all you need to do is simply sew all the elements together.

Legs

1 To make the legs, take the lavender blue chenille stem, 1cm (⅜in) in diameter, and cut a length about 21cm (8¼in) long to give you enough stem for both legs and a section in-between to attach to the fairy's lower body.

2 Bend the stem around a pencil in the middle to create a curve for the top section of the legs, to be attached to the pompom body.

3 For the feet, bend the stem 2.5cm (1in) in from each end. With the sharp pair of scissors, trim the ends of the feet into little wedge shapes, then, with the needle-nose pliers, curl over the ends.

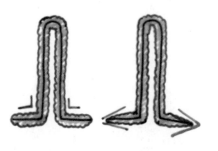

Equipment and Materials

Needle-nose pliers

Small, sharp pair of scissors

Pompom discs: medium, 3.5cm (1⅜in) diameter, and small, 2cm (¾in) in diameter

Sewing needle and thread (lavender)

Permanent marker pen

Felt-tip pen (pink)

50g ball of wool (lavender, shiny finish)

1 chenille stem, 30cm x 1cm (12in x ⅜in) (lavender blue)

1 chenille stem, 30cm x 5mm (12in x ¼in) (lavender blue)

1 chenille stem, about 8cm x 5mm (3⅛in x ¼in) (glittery purple)

1 commercially made pompom, 1cm (⅜in) (flesh-coloured, peach, beige or brown)

1 commercially made pompom, 3mm (⅛in) (lavender)

1 sheet of 13cm (5⅛in) square of transparent or opaque plastic

Back view

Actual size 170mm (6⅝in) from tip
of the antennae to the end of the tail

4 Shape the feet and heels, then contour the
   lower leg by trimming away the pile from
   the chenille stem until you are happy with
   the shape.

5 Bend the knees 4cm (1½in) up from the
   bottom of the heel. Shape the upper calf
   of the leg as well.

Arms

1 To make the four arms, take the other thick lavender blue chenille
   stem, and cut four lengths of at least 4.5cm (1¾in). As a guide, Matte
   Moth fairy's arms are a little thinner than those of Berry fairy.

2 Create the arms by taking the small chenille stems and curling
   over the ends. Using the sharp scissors, trim into shape.

3 To make the wrists, trim indentations above the hand. For the
   elbow, bend the stem arm 2cm (¾in) up from the bottom of
   the hand.

4 Make a loop at the top of the arm, ready to attach. Make four
   identical arms following this method. Set the prepared legs and
   arms aside until you have made the pompom body.

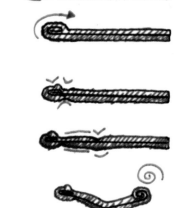

Body

1 Using the medium-sized pompom disc and lavender wool, create a
   pompom for the upper body. Trim off any long, straggling threads, but
   avoid cutting the pile back too drastically as Matte Moth fairy has a
   loose-textured surface and requires less three-dimensional weaving.

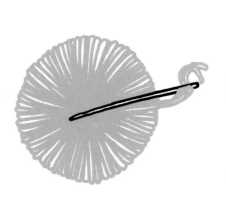

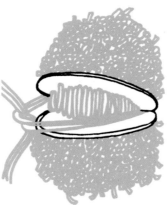

2 Find the central thread of the pompom body, and establish which is the top and bottom. You want the pompom body to be bottom heavy, like a pear. Sometimes a pompom naturally has one side larger than the other anyway, but to work the right shape, you need to do some sculpting. Trim some of the surface thread away from the top shoulder area of the pompom body.

3 To create the soft, wispy surface, weave additional thread through the pompom, and trim the ends of the thread 5mm (¼in) from the surface of the pompom.

Head

1 Create the pompom head using both small pompom discs. To retain the same softness as the body, do not trim away the outer surface of the pompom with the exception of long, straggly bits.

2 Position the commercially made pompom face onto the pompom head. Open up the pile of the pompom head a little and nestle the pompom face into the bottom part of it. Using a needle and thread, sew the face into the pompom head using needle and sewing thread.

3 Position the pompom head and body together and use the lavender wool to sew into place.

Tail

1 Using one side of the small pompom discs only and the same lavender wool, make five pompoms. You want to create smaller pompoms here than for the head, so do not wrap the wool too densely around the disc.

2 If you find the size of the tail pompoms too similar to that of the head, trim around the circumference of each, gradually removing the pile until you have an even coverage.

3 Line the tail pompoms in a row, and with a needle and lavender thread, sew them into the pompom body. Pull tightly on the wool thread as you work to secure the joins between each. Weave through the entire length of the body with the lavender wool to reinforce the connection between the pompoms and build up a three-dimensionally woven network into the fabric of Matte Moth fairy.

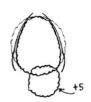

Antennae

1 To create a pair of antennae for Matte Moth fairy, take a glittery purple chenille stem, about 8cm (3⅛in) long, and trim the pile down almost to the wire.

2 Using the needle-nose pliers, pinch the ends to twist them around into a curl. Bend the antennae wire in the middle.

3 Using the lavender wool, attach the antennae to the top of the back of the head.

4 To create a simple hairpiece, once you have attached the antennae, sew a loop of lavender wool to stand up between them on the top of the head.

Wings

1 Take a piece of opaque plastic, 13cm (5⅛in) square, and using a sharp pair of scissors, cut a pair of wings for Matte Moth fairy from the wing template patterns (see Techniques, page 18).

2 Sew the wings onto the back of the fairy.

Finishing touches

1 Refine any unfinished areas by trimming with the sharp scissors and, if necessary, by weaving three-dimensionally with the lavender thread.

2 Using a needle and lavender thread, attach the legs to the bottom of the pompom body. Open up the pile at the bottom of the pompom body, and push the leg loop into the pile of the pompom. Sew into place.

3 Attach the two pairs of arms at the top and sides of the body pompom. Position the top pair at shoulder level just under the head pompom, and the second pair 1cm (⅜in) below, in the mid-tummy region.

4 Add a tiny commercially made 3mm (⅛in) lavender blue pompom for the nose to the centre of the face. Using a needle and lavender sewing thread, sew it into position.

5 Take a permanent ink marker and dot a pair of eyes just above, and to either side of, the pompom nose.

6 To create a pretty blush to the cheeks of the fairy, gently add a touch of pink water-based felt-tip marker to the fairy's face. Be careful to not apply it too heavily as it can spoil the fairy's features.

Matte Moth fairy assembly map

This assembly map illustrates all components and stages required to make your own Matte Moth fairy.

Acorn fairy

Acorn fairy's tiny, nut-brown body has a smooth finish and a little tail created with additional woven thread. I have used a cashmere-mix wool which gives the pompoms a delicate finish. A small pair of embroidery scissors is useful for shaping the pompoms as these work much better with the wool. Cashmere wool is really great for this project, but is quite expensive, so always keep your eyes peeled for bargains — I bought mine from a mixed bin of wool and it cost hardly anything.

Legs

1 To begin, make a pair of legs from the 30cm (12in) lavender chenille stem. This fairy's arms and legs are quite long, so for the legs you need to cut a length 20cm (7⅞in) long.

2 Bend the stem in the middle to create a curve, ready to join to the pompom body.

3 To make the feet, bend the ends of the stems about 3cm (1¼in) in, at a 90° angle.

4 Trim away the pile at the tips of the feet into a wedge shape to create the toes. Use the needle-nose pliers to twist them into a curl.

5 With the scissors, trim away the pile to make the soles of the feet, then, to create the knees, clip an indentation in each leg, just over 3cm (1¼in) from the heel. Clip away some of the pile with the scissors on the back of both knees to create the indentations.

Equipment and Materials

Needle-nose pliers

Sewing needle

Embroidery scissors

Permanent marker pen

Pompom discs: medium, 3.5cm (1⅜in) in diameter, and small, 2cm (¾in) in diameter

25g ball of wool with a cashmere content (nut brown)

25g ball of wool with a cashmere content (two-tone cream and beige)

1 tiny commercially made 3mm (⅛in) pompom (flesh-coloured)

1 commercially made pompom 1cm (⅜in) in diameter (flesh-coloured)

1 chenille stem 30cm x 1cm (12in x ⅜in) (lavender)

1 chenille stem 30cm x 5mm (12in x ¼in) (flesh-coloured)

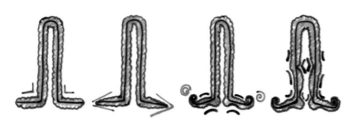

Actual size
135mm (5⅓in)
from tip of
antennae to the
heel

Back view

6 Shape the calf and thigh areas by trimming away the surface of the pile. Be careful not to remove too much material. Bend the knees into position where you have created the bend.

7 Once the legs are trimmed into shape, set them aside until the pompom body is ready.

Arms

1 Cut a 13cm (5⅛in) length from the 30cm (12in) flesh-coloured stem.

2 To begin the arms, cut two 6cm (2⅜in) lengths and use the needle-nose pliers to curl over one end of each a couple of times to create the hands. The two complete arms should measure about 5cm (2in) long from the top of the arms to the hands.

3 Using the embroidery scissors, trim indentations for the wrists. To form the inner side of the arm, trim away a little of the pile on one side about 1.5cm (⅝in) up from the wrist, to the elbow.

4 Refine the shape of the arms. As you adjust, remove only a small amount of pile at a time to ensure that you do not overwork them.

5 Make a loop at the armpit end of the stem arms to attach to the pompom body at a later stage.

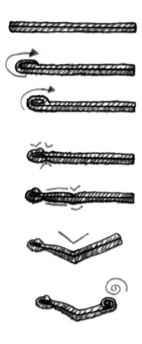

Body

1 To begin Acorn fairy's body, take the medium-sized pompoms discs and, using the nut-brown wool, make a pompom.

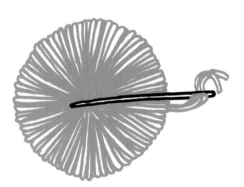

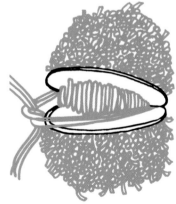

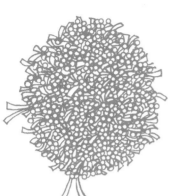
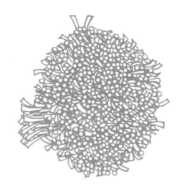
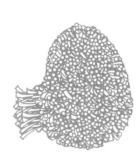

2 Take the medium-sized pompom and find the central thread, which should be on the horizontal to enable you to establish the top and bottom of the pompom. Begin trimming away the surface of the pompom, gradually shaping it until you form a fat kidney-bean shape. Do not remove any pile from the fairy's bottom, to leave a bump for the tail.

3 As you carve and sculpt with your scissors, weave in additional thread to the bump shape to build it up into a bulky shape. Weaving more thread into the body of the pompom consolidates the structure.

4 Build up the upper chest area with additional thread, and round out the upper shoulder. If you wish, alter the length of the body by adding and trimming the pile at a greater length at the top or bottom of the pompom.

5 As you work, try to aim for the following approximate proportions: the pompom body measures just less than 4cm (1½in) in height, the middle of the tummy section about 2.5cm (1in), and the chest area about 2cm (¾in) in diameter.

6 When the body shaping is nearly complete, place the legs into the bottom of the body pompom fitting them into the pile as far as possible. Attach them into the body using a needle and a length of nut-brown wool.

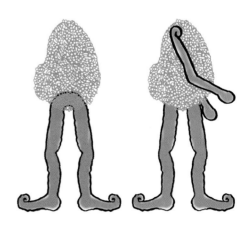

7 Using the needle and nut-brown wool, attach the two arms to the shoulders through the upper arm loops.

Head

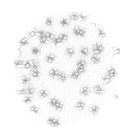

1 Make a second, smaller pompom for the head using the two-tone cream and beige wool. If you cannot find a two-tone wool, make your own by threading the craft needle with two different coloured wools at the same time. It will give you a good patchy, mottled texture.

2 To make the head shape, take the small pompom and trim away the surface to reduce its overall size. Although it is not necessary to follow the exact measurements when making your fairy, the head should end up about 2.5cm (1in) in diameter.

3 Using the embroidery scissors, trim off some of the pompom pile to create an acorn-shaped head.

4 Now create a neck for the pompom head to rest on. Position two flesh-coloured commercially made pompoms 5mm (¼in) in diameter, to the centre of the top of the pompom body. Sew these two stacked pompoms together and attach them into the pile of the pompom.

5 Insert the pompom face into the pile of the bottom half of the head. Make sure that the point of the acorn rests at the top of the head, slightly tilted to the back.

6 For the nose, position a tiny commercially made 3mm (⅛in) flesh-coloured pompom onto the middle of the face. Sew into place, just below the halfway point, with a needle and sewing thread.

Antennae

1 To create a pair of antennae, cut a 6cm (2⅜in) length of the same flesh-coloured chenille stem from which you made the arms.

2 Clip the pile down almost to the wire.

3 Using the needle-nose pliers, twist a curl at either end of the stem. Bend the stem in the middle and ensure that both curls point out to the side in opposite directions.

4 Attach the antennae to the middle of the top of Acorn fairy's head. Sew into place using sewing needle and thread.

Finishing touches

1 Using a permanent marker pen, dot two eyes above and to each side of the nose.

2 Acorn fairy is not designed to have wings, but if you want to decorate her further, there is plenty of scope to do so. Add a piece of lace or craft felt around her neck, for example, or make her some brightly coloured slippers.

Acorn fairy assembly map

This assembly map illustrates all components and stages required to make Acorn fairy.

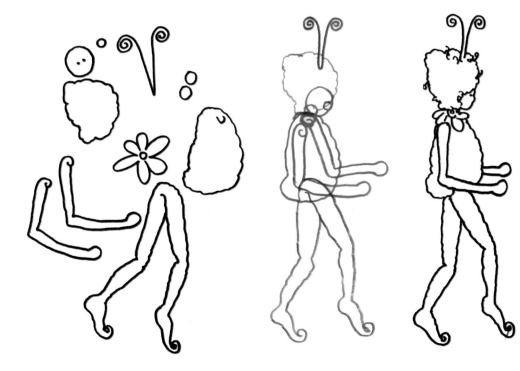

Lily fairy

Lily fairy is a dainty little fairy with soft, pale colouring. She is unadorned with the exception of her pompom head which is a profusion of raspberry-textured woven wool bobbles. She is a great fairy to have fun with – you can embellish her with lace or ribbons, or dress her in handmade fairy clothes.

Legs

1 Begin Lily fairy's legs by cutting a 16cm (6¼in) length from a pale or sage green chenille stem.

2 Bend the stem in the middle to create a curve to attach to the fairy's pompom body.

3 To make the feet, bend the ends of the stems about 2cm (¾in) in, at a 90° angle.

4 Trim away the pile at the tip of the feet into a wedge shape to create the toes. Use the needle-nose pliers to twist them into a curl over the top.

5 With the scissors, trim pile away from the soles of the feet, then clip an indentation for each knee in the legs, 3cm (1¼in) in from the heel. Clip away some of the pile with the scissors at the back of both knees to shape a bend. The upper thigh should measure about 2.5cm (1in) long, disappearing into the pile of the pompom body. You can vary the lengths to change the style of the legs.

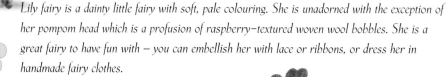

Lily fairy

Back view

Actual size
110mm (4¼in) from
the tip of the
antennae to the heel

53

6   Shape the calf and thigh areas by trimming away the surface of the pile. Be careful not to remove too much, unless you want to create a spindly appearance. Bend the knees into position where you have created an indentation.

7   Once the legs are trimmed into shape, set them aside until the pompom body is ready.

Arms

1   Make a pair of arms by taking a 10cm (4in) length flesh-coloured chenille stem. Lily fairy's arms measure about 4cm (1½in) long; add an extra amount for the loops that attach the shoulder to the pompom body. Create the arms simultaneously, ensuring that they are the same length and shape as you work; it is harder to remember these little steps further on in the process.

2   Create a curl at the end of each stem arm for the hands.

3   Trim and carve the wrists and elbows to get the desired effect.

4   Make the loops at the armpits to attach to the pompom body later on.

5   Set aside the legs and arms until the pompom body is made.

Body

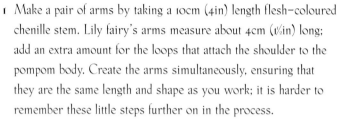

1   To create the pompom body, take the shiny white wool or cotton thread, and wind it around the medium-sized pompom disc. Use one half of the disc only and do not overfill it. The wool's cotton content helps to reduce the size of the pompom because the thread has less spring.

2   Once the pompom body is complete, find the central thread and establish the top and bottom of the pompom.

3   You are aiming for a kidney-bean shape, flat at the chest and sloping down towards a rounded tummy and bottom. Take a sharp pair of scissors, and begin to trim the pompom body, starting with the sides. Remove some the pile from the middle section of the pompom, taking care not to cut through the central thread. Lily fairy has only the slightest definition to her waist. Leave some of the pile on her bottom to create a rounded bump at the back, and more around her tummy. Once complete, Lily fairy should measure 3cm (1½in) in height and about 2cm (¾in) around the middle.

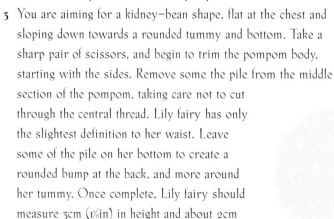

4 The pompom pile is always more dense at the sides of the pompoms, but weave additional thread to the top and bottom areas of the pompom body, until it is blended in.

5 Insert the legs into the pile of the bottom of the pompom body. Sew them in with the white cotton thread. Fill in any thin areas of pile with the white wool.

6 Place the arms directly into the sides of the shoulders of the pompom body. Sew them into the pompom body with the same white thread.

7 Once the arms and legs are in place, the shape can be refined. Add more thread where necessary and trim away the excess. Continue to add and trim until you are happy with the overall effect. The three-dimensionally woven thread should pass through all of the regions of the body pompom to create a solid structure.

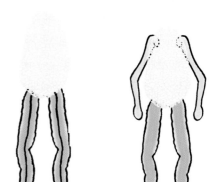

Head

1 Create Lily fairy's pompom head with the 2cm (¾in) pompom discs using a pale peach or pink wool. This pompom needs to have quite a bit of its surface pile removed to make it as small as possible. Wind the disc with less wool than for the body to create a smaller pompom.

2 Using a small, sharp pair of scissors, trim the surface of the pompom head, removing an even layer of the pile until you almost reach the central thread.

3 Set the commercially made 1cm (⅜in) flesh-coloured pompom face into the handmade pompom head. Embed the smaller pompom face into the bottom of pompom head so that it has a large quantity of the pile sitting on top and behind it. Sew this into position with a sewing needle and flesh-coloured or white thread.

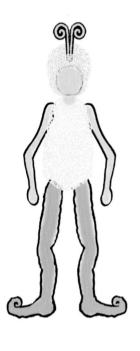

4 When the face and head are attached and in the correct position, begin to weave in additional thread to the surface of the head as though you are embroidering it. Do not cut it away as you usually do when three-dimensional weaving, leave the little loops of hair sticking out just above the surface to create a bobbly texture. Apply this technique to the entire hair area, making slightly fuller loops at the side of the face, at the neckline.

5 Before attaching the pompom head to the pompom body, make the neck. With your needle and thread, sew together two commercially made 5mm (¼in) pompoms and connect both to the top of the body pompom.

6 Position a 1cm (⅜in) flesh-coloured commercially made pompom into the top of the body pompom on the back side. Embed this pompom into the pile of the top of the torso shape by separating the pile fibres to make room for it. Weave and fill in any bare areas with the white pompom thread.

7 Attach the head and face to the top of the neck. Ensure that the needle passes through some parts of the pompom body to secure the join.

Antennae

1 Take a 5cm (2in) length of cotton-covered stem in a pale pink or peach and trim away the pile from the surface almost down to the wire.

2 Using the needle-nose pliers, pinch each end to create a curl. Bend the wire in the middle to complete the antennae.

3 Once you have completed the hair, and using needle and sewing thread, add the antennae by sewing into the centre of the pompom head, positioning them near to the face, about 7mm (⅜in) off.

Wings

1 Cut out a wing shape following the template (see Techniques, page 19) and pierce holes to attach to the fairy.

2 Overlap the two separate wing pieces slightly when attaching to the back of Lily fairy. Sew them into the body with the sewing needle and thread.

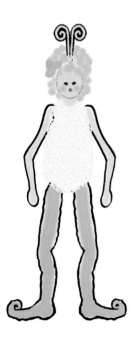

Finishing touches

1 To create the facial features, use your pair of sharp scissors and clip away a tiny indentation in the centre of the face to make a space for the eyes.

2 Use a black permanent pen to apply two dots for eyes, 3mm (⅛in) apart, into the contours of the eyes in the centre of the face. Make a red permanent pen dot to form a mouth underneath the eyes.

3 Delicately blush the cheeks using a water-based felt-tip pen.

4 To add a rosette to Lily fairy's hair, cut out a small oblong of green craft felt. Gather into a rosette shape, then position into the hair and sew into place. Cut the ankle flowers from the same material and slip onto the feet.

Lily fairy assembly map

This assembly map illustrates all components and stages required to make Lily fairy.

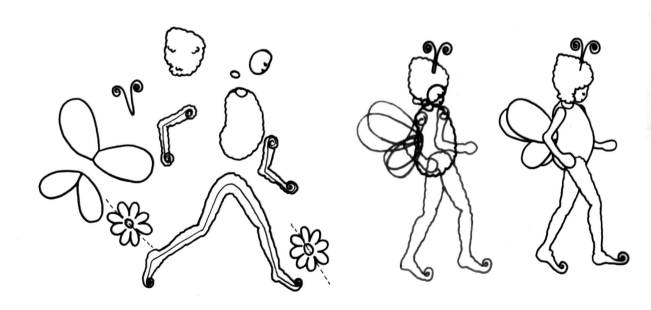

Dragonfly fairy

Dragonfly fairy is the most glamorous, and indeed, complex of the fairy projects to make, but very satisfying. She requires three-dimensional weaving to build up the areas around the neck, arms and tail, and trimming with small craft scissors to achieve her unique, extended body shape.

Legs

1 To begin the Dragonfly fairy project, make a pair of legs. Take a thick flesh-coloured or pale pink chenille stem and cut a 20cm (7⅞in) length.

2 Bend the chenille stem in the middle to create a curve, then bend both ends of the stem, 3cm (1¼in) in, for each foot.

3 Using a pair of sharp scissors, clip a wedge shape to make the toes.

4 Use the needle-nose pliers to clip the end of the stems and bend them over to create the curl at the end of each foot. Shape the soles of the feet, too, by carefully trimming them. Work both feet simultaneously so that they match.

5 With the craft scissors, begin to shape the legs. First trim indentations in the ankles, then clip away a V shape to create the knees. Trim away a small amount of material from the upper leg sections to give definition to the thighs. Finally, bend the legs into position at the knee.

Equipment and Materials

Needle-nose pliers

Small, sharp pair of scissors

Cutting pliers or utility scissors

Permanent marker pen

Pompom discs: medium, 3.5 cm (1⅜in) in diameter, and small, 2cm (¾in) in diameter

50g ball of wool (multicoloured)

Wool (for sewing)

Needles

2 chenille stems, 30cm x 1cm (12in x ⅜in) (flesh-coloured)

1 chenille stem about 3cm (1¼in) long (metallic purple)

1 commercially made pompom, 1cm (⅜in) in diameter (flesh-coloured, peach, beige or brown)

1 commercially made pompom, 2cm (¾in) in diameter (glittery purple)

1 commercially made pompom, 1cm (⅜in) in diameter (glittery purple)

3 commercially made pompoms, 3mm (⅛in) in diameter (flesh-coloured)

3 commercially made pompoms, 5mm (¼in) in diameter (flesh-coloured)

1 sheet 8cm (3⅛in) square transparent or opaque plastic

Dragonfly fairy

Back view

Actual size
115mm (4¹/₂in) from
the tip of the
antennae to the heel

Arms

1   To make the arms, use the same flesh-coloured chenille stem as you have for the legs. Cut two lengths of stem 5.5cm (2⅛in) long.

2   To make the hands, use the needle-nose pliers to curl and loop over the ends of each stem. The final hands should measure about 1cm (⅜in) in length. Trim the hands slightly to give them a better shape.

3   Shape the wrist by trimming little indentations into the stem just above the hand. Shape the lower arm and cut a V shape into the middle of each on one side, about 2cm (¾in) from the wrist.

4   If necessary, finishing carving and refining the hands until you are happy with them.

5   The upper arm is slightly shorter than the lower arm and hand. Leave some pile at the elbow on the outer edge of the arm so that it protrudes outwards. Make a loop at the end of the arm. Trim and shape the upper arm to add definition.

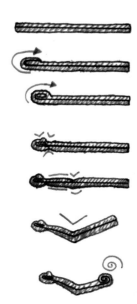

Body

1   Dragonfly fairy has a few areas that require three-dimensional weaving. Build up the chest, neck and tops of the arms with additional thread. The thickest part of the pompom is the middle section around the central thread. Adding thread horizontally through the thinner sections ensures a more even distribution of pile.

2   Using the multicoloured wool and one half of the medium-sized disc only, create the pompom body.

3   Trim away any loose ends. Find the central thread of the pompom and keep it horizontal to establish the top and bottom.

4   Now shape the body. Dragonfly fairy has a narrow chest and slightly rounded tummy. Like some of the other fairies, her body is a kidney-bean shape, but is longer and more tubular. The torso should measure just less than 4cm (1⅝in) in height. Keep this in mind as you work.

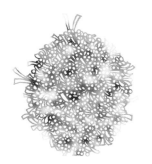

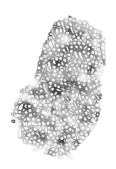
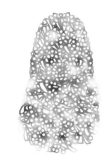

Side view   Front view

Using a sharp pair of scissors, carefully trim away this area. Trim the torso by removing a section from the centre of the pompom, then create a waist by trimming around this shape. Leave a bump at the back lower half of the pompom for the bottom, another at the middle for the tummy and a further two discreet bumps at the chest. Once complete, you should have a slight indentation between the tummy and chest.

5 Refine this basic shape until you are happy with it.

6 As the weaving and trimming process progresses, the body becomes more dense with the added thread. It becomes easier to enhance the design if the arms and legs are in place, so first fit the legs snugly into the bottom of the pompom body. To secure them into the fabric, sew into position with multicoloured wool and weave it through the entire length of the body.

7 Position the arms onto the sides of the top section of the pompom. Attach them with the multicoloured wool, and to secure, weave the needle through the other areas of the body.

Tip When shaping the pompom body, be careful to avoid cutting the central thread by mistake, particularly early on in the development of the pompom-shaping process. It is less hazardous later on when the three-dimensional weaving is well underway because the network of fibres ensures that the pompom remains safely intact.

Tail

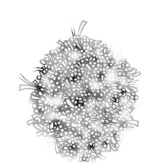

1 To create Dragonfly fairy's tail section, make four small multi-coloured pompoms using the small-sized pompom disc and the multicoloured wool.

2 Attach them to the lower back section of the body pompom in a line. Keep the central threads in a horizontal position when adding the pompoms to each other with the needle and thread. Pull tightly on the needle and thread to press the joins between them.

3 To create the curl in the tail, thread your needle through the length of the tail back and forth a couple of times, then, to press the shape together, pull on the thread tightly to draw the end of the tail into an upward position.

4 Pin this shape into position by sewing the thread into the end of the tail section and securing it tightly. This process is a tiny bit tricky, so you may have to repeat it in order to get enough of a curve into the tail. Thread through the centre of the tail to the body a few times to ensure a secure join between all body parts.

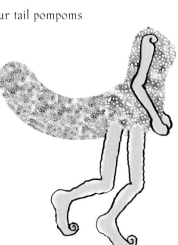

5 Fill in the little joins between the four tail pompoms by weaving extra thread three-dimensionally into them, and trimming the tail into a tubular structure. This adding and trimming process will take you a little time, but gives a smooth, precise finish to the piece. If you wish to refine the finish of the tail further, cut tiny ridges into the underneath of the tail.

Head

1 To create the head, take one of the 2cm (¾in) glittery purple commercially made pompoms and position a second, 1cm (⅜in) pompom of the same variety, to the top back of the pompom head. Sew them together using a needle and some wool thread.

2 To create the face, position a pink or flesh-coloured 1cm (⅜in) pompom onto the pompom head and embed it into the pile of the glittery purple pompom head. Sew into place using flesh-coloured sewing thread.

3 Take the 3mm (⅛in) commercially made flesh-coloured pompom, and sew into place halfway down the face. If you would like to add ears to the fairy, attach the tiny pompom ears to each side at about eye level.

4 Take two 5mm (¼in) commercially made pompoms and sew them together with thread to create the neck shape. Sew a third 5mm (¼in) pompom into the pile of the top front of the neck area. This acts as an anchor or platform on which to rest the two neck pompoms. Attach the neck pompoms to it by sewing them together.

5 Sew the glittery purple head onto the neck. Fill any patchy areas with the multicoloured wool and trim to refine the shape around the neck and base pompoms until you are happy with them.

Antennae

1 Create the antennae from a 3cm (1¼in) length of metallic purple chenille stem. Trim down the stem to narrow the width.

2 Using the needle-nose pliers, pinch the ends to bend them into a curl shape.

3 Using a needle and thread, add the antennae by sewing them onto the top of head.

Wings

1 Following the Dragonfly wing pattern template (see Techniques, page 19), create the wings. These are the largest wings of all and suit the extended shape of Dragonfly fairy very well.

2 Attach by sewing into the back of Dragonfly Fairy. She's now ready to take off!

Finishing touches

Use a permanent marker pen to dot the eyes just above and to the sides of the nose.

Dragonfly fairy assembly map

This assembly map illustrates all components required to make your very own Dragonfly fairy.

The Creatures

Basking in a sun-warmed home
Blackbird sings after springtime rain
Lilac-scented wind fills the air
His call so bright brings friends home again

Grasshopper

The grasshopper is a very jolly character, and can be completed in a variety of colour and design combinations. I include only one design here, but once you have made one, you can develop lots of ideas for more grasshopper friends. This is an accessible project, and makes use of sewing, bending, shaping and trimming techniques.

Body and head

1 To begin making the grasshopper, line up the five body and head pompoms in a row, positioning the two smallest pompoms at either end.

2 To create flattish surface joins between the pompoms, clip away a little from the sides of each, with the exception of the pompom head.

3 Set the pompoms in an semicircular shape, then take your needle and green thread, and sew them together. To make the eyes, take the two tiny purple, beige or blue pompoms and sew them into position onto the pompom head.

Tip When selecting the five pompoms for the body, make sure that the two end pompoms are of similar size, and that they are smaller in diameter compared to the three middle body pompoms.

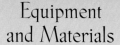
Equipment and Materials

Needle-nose pliers

Sewing needle

Sewing thread (green)

Small craft scissors

1 pipe cleaner or chenille stem, full length, 5mm (¼in) wide (bright green)

2 pipe cleaners or chenille stems, each 23cm x 5mm (9⅛in x ¼in) (bright yellow)

1 pipe cleaner or chenille stem, 23cm x 5mm (9⅛in x ¼in) (bright turquoise)

3 commercially made pompoms, 1cm (⅜in) in diameter (dark green)

2 commercially made pompoms, 7mm (¼in) in diameter (dark green)

2 commercially made pompoms, 3mm (⅛in) (purple, beige or blue)

*Actual size 40mm
(1½in) from the nose to
the tail*

Wings and back plate

1 To create the wings, take a 23cm (9⅛in) long bright turquoise chenille stem, and trim away the pile from the surface, almost down to the wire.

2 To prepare the stems for the antennae and the back plate, trim down the two same-length yellow chenille stems in a similar way.

3 For the backplate, take a section up to 10cm (4in) long, of one of the trimmed yellow pipe cleaners, and use the needle-nose pliers to bend the end into a curly coil shape. Bend the curl around a couple of times. Following the diagram, repeat this bending and curling process three times, until you achieve the pretzel-like shape. Keep the curls tight, as the back plate sits on top of the grasshopper's back to cover the wings; if the coils are too large, they will not fit into this small area.

4 To create the wing shape, take a 5cm (2in) length of the trimmed turquoise pipe cleaner, and using the needle-nose pliers, pinch the end of the stem and bend it around to make a curl at one end. As before, bend this curl around a couple of times. Repeat this with the other end of the stem. Each curled end should meet in the middle of the stem.

5 Take another 5cm (2in) length of turquoise blue chenille stem, and make a second wing.

6 Fit the yellow back plate to the top of the wings, using a needle and green sewing thread to mount them into position.

> Tip Bends and curves are difficult with these tiny wing and back plate shapes. Keep the folds tightly curled by using the fine end of the needle-nose pliers.

Legs

1 To create the first pair of the three leg sections, take the bright green 30cm (12in) long pipe cleaner and cut one length 10cm (4in) long. These form the grasshopper's back legs, each 5cm (2in) long.

2 Starting at one end of the stem, trim away the pile almost down to the wire from half of its length.

3 Use your scissors to carefully trim away a nicely rounded end to the fuller end of the stem. With the needle-nose pliers, pinch the skinny end into a curl.

4 Bend the stem leg in the middle to pose the leg into the correct shape. Repeat this process for the second long leg.

5 To make each of the middle pair of legs, take a 6.5cm (2½in) length of another bright green pipe cleaner, and trim away to remove much of the pile from two-thirds of the length of the stem, almost to the wire. Wind the end into a curl as you have before. Repeat this for the remaining leg.

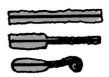

6 For each of the third and final pair of legs, take another length of pipe cleaner about 2.5cm (1in) long, and trim away the pile, almost down to the wire, so that the entire length is thin and velvety in texture. Wind one end into a curl. Repeat this for the remaining leg.

7 Once the legs are complete, attach them in pairs to either side of the grasshopper's body with needle and sewing thread. Form tiny loops at the top end of each leg to help you attach them securely. Fix the longest legs at the back of the grasshopper, the smaller, semi-trimmed legs to the middle body section, and finally, the skinny legs to the front.

Antennae

1 To create the antennae, take an 7cm (2¾in) length of trimmed yellow pipe cleaner and, using the needle-nose pliers, pinch the end of the stem to wind it into a curl. Repeat this with the other end of the stem. Fold the stem in the middle to create the two antennae. If necessary, adjust the curl with the needle-nose pliers.

2 Sew the antennae into position onto the top of the grasshopper's head.

Grasshopper assembly map

This assembly map illustrates all components and stages required to make your very own grasshopper.

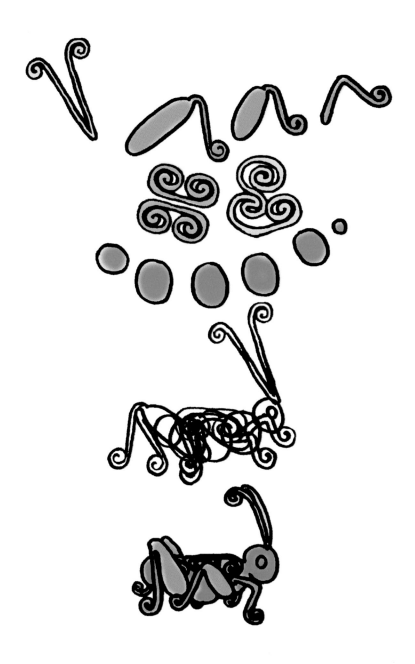

 # Baby bird

Baby bird is the cutest and most accessible of the pompom birds to make. There is no three-dimensional weaving or sculpting to be done, and once the pompoms are joined together, it is simply a matter of attaching them with some sewing thread. Additional elements, such as the claw-shaped feet and wings, made from pipe cleaners, are also very simple to achieve.

Tip You can substitute the commercially made pompoms with handmade ones, but remember to maintain the same proportions given in the instructions.

Body, head and tail

1 To start creating Baby bird, collect all the beige or brown pompoms required for the body, five in total. Take one of the small 2.5cm (1in) pompoms and using a pair of scissors, trim away a little from one edge to create a flattened surface to join to another pompom. This forms baby bird's tail end.

2 Take the larger 4cm (1⅝in) pompom, which will form the body, and fix the pompom tail onto the bottom of one side with a needle and some sewing thread.

Equipment and Materials

Sewing needle

Thread

Small, sharp pair of scissors

Needle-nose pliers

1 commercially made pompom, 4cm (1⅝in) in diameter (beige or brown)

2 commercially made pompoms, 2.5cm (1in) in diameter (beige or brown)

2 commercially made pompoms, 5mm (¼in) in diameter (brown or black)

3 chenille stems, 30cm x 5mm (12in x ¼in) (beige or brown)

1 pipe cleaner, 10cm (4in) long (beige, brown, black or green)

1 pipe cleaner, 3cm (1¼in) long (white)

*Actual size 50mm (2in) from
the top of the head to the
bottom of the chest*

Back view

3 Take the second 2.5cm (1in) pompom and sew it to the pompom tail and body. It should be slightly raised at the front.

4 Sew two small 5mm (¼in) pompoms to the pompom head, one on either side, to form Baby bird's eyes.

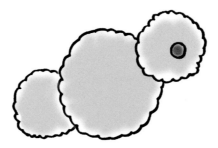

Beak

1 To create the beak, take a 2cm (¾in) long white pipe cleaner, and curl one end into a loop. Repeat this at the other end of the stem.

2 Bend this section in the middle to create a bent V-shaped beak.

3 Position the beak at about eye level on the pompom head, and sew it securely through the two loops.

Clawed feet

1 To create the clawed feet, take a 10cm (4in) long pipe cleaner in your preferred colour (either beige, brown, black or green) and trim away the pile until almost down to the wire.

2 Bend each end of the stem, about 7mm (⅜in) in, into a V shape, then make three same-sized folds. Bend the stem of the final fold under the first fold to secure the foot shape.

3 Bend the middle of the stem into a curve to attach to the underside of the bird, and sew into the pile of the pompoms with needle and thread, between the tail and body.

Wings

1 To create Baby bird's wings, take a beige or brown chenille stem, 30cm (12in) long, and loop over at both ends to make them safe.

2 Bend the stem in the middle, then fold back each side into a wing shape.

3 Wrap the looped ends over the outer stem of the wing, on either side of its pointed-nose shape, and under again to secure it. Pinch the tips of the wings into shape and pull out gently to create a wing span on each side.

4 Take another chenille stem in the same colour and loop one end around the outer side. Weave the stem through the inner and outer span of the wing, filling it in as you work.

5 Wind the stem over the nose of the wing and continue weaving the chenille stem through the other wing. You will need to use a second stem to finish filling in.

6 Once complete, attach the wings to the back of Baby bird, just below the seam between the head and body, using needle and sewing thread. Overlap the wings slightly, to adjust the fit. To help stabilize Baby bird when it is placed in a standing position, curl the very tips of the wings.

Baby bird assembly map

These diagrams illustrate the components and stages required to make your very own
Baby bird.

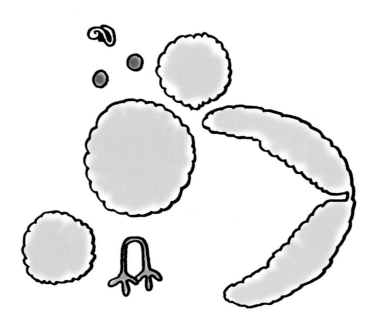

Blackbird

Blackbird is a dramatic figure in the fairy and creature landscape, with his shiny, black wings and beady eyes. He may be a little more complex to make, but is very rewarding. The most challenging aspect is the wing span, but once you have the basic technique, you will be able to create all kinds of different birds.

Body, head and tail

1 Begin the project by making two small handmade pompoms for the head and tail part of the bird. You will need to use two small 2cm (¾in) pompom discs and the black wool thread (see Techniques, page 10). If you want to add some detail, vary the colour of the thread underneath where the beak will be positioned. To do this, wind a different-coloured wool around a quarter of the disc for the pompom head.

2 Make a third pompom using the medium-sized 3.5cm (1⅜in) discs to create the body section of the bird.

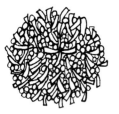

Equipment and Materials

Needle-nose pliers

Sewing and craft needles

Small pair of craft scissors

Pompom discs: medium, 3.5cm (1⅜in) in diameter, and small, 2cm (¾in) in diameter

25g ball of wool, preferably with a knobbly texture (black)

8–10 cotton chenille stems or pipe cleaners, 23cm x 5mm (9⅛in x ¼in) (black)

1 cotton chenille stem, 23cm x 5mm (9⅛in x ¼in) (brown)

2 tiny commercially made pompoms, 5mm (¼in) in diameter (brown)

Blackbird

*Actual size 65mm (2½in)
from the top of the head to
the bird's clawed feet.*

3 Find the central thread on the medium-sized pompom, and positioning it vertically, embed the two smaller pompoms into the pile at either side of it. If you are adding a different colour to the bird's chin, position it so that this section rests just under the halfway mark on the head.

4 Sew the pompoms firmly together, by passing the needle through the centre of the body pompom with the black wool.

5 Once joined together, begin to sculpt the pompom to which the tail will be attached. Using a pair of scissors, trim away the pile to create a slightly truncated end.

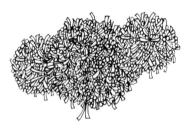 

Wings

1 The wing is the most challenging part of this project. To create the wing span for the bird, take a black 25cm (9⅞in) long chenille stem or pipe cleaner. Bend a curve in the centre of the stem and then bend a bow shape with the two ends to create Blackbird's wing span.

2 Loop over the ends over to cover the sharp points. These will blend in and form the end feathers of the wing.

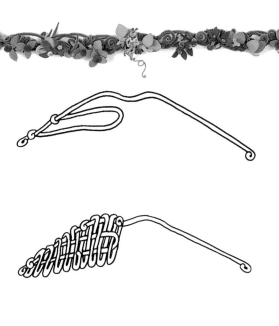

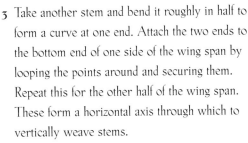

3 Take another stem and bend it roughly in half to form a curve at one end. Attach the two ends to the bottom end of one side of the wing span by looping the points around and securing them. Repeat this for the other half of the wing span. These form a horizontal axis through which to vertically weave stems.

4 To create the effect of feathers across the wings, take another stem and loop the point of one end around the tip of the outer side of the left wing span. Weave the stem up and down through the stem forming the horizontal axis, until you have created a tightly meshed framework. Fold the final point over to secure. Repeat the procedure for the right wing. Make sure that the left and right wings remain separate pieces to emulate the realistic movement of a bird.

5 The wings should follow a slight curve across the back of the bird's body. Using the black thread, sew the wings to the very centre of the top edge of the bird's pompom body, just below the pompom head.

Tail

1 The tail consists of three layers of pipe cleaners, bent into feather-like folds like a concertina, which can then be attached to the end of the pompom tail with wool thread. To make the top layer, bend a black chenille stem into three spokes, each measuring 2.5cm (1in) long.

2 Create a second, bottom layer for the tail, by bending four concertina folds each measuring 4cm (1⅝in) long.

3 The middle layer weaves the top and bottom layers together. Take another stem and weave it through the two, looping and binding them together. The top layer of the tail should have the shorter concertina folds resting over top of the bottom layer with the longer concertina folds. Loop over the ends to cover the sharp points of the stems.

4 Attach the tail feathers to the end of the pompom tail, fitting it snugly into the pile, and sew them in with black thread.

Beak

1 To create the beak, take a 5cm (2in) length of black chenille stem and curl over both ends to create a loop. Bend the stem in half and form into a beak-like curve.

2 Attach the beak to the front centre of the pompom head using the black thread. If you have also used a second colour, position the beak on that colour break.

3 Fill in the open middle section of the beak, by winding black wool around the surface and securing through the front and sides of the bird's face.

Clawed feet

1 To create the clawed feet, take a brown 23cm (9⅛in) long stem and fold it in half.

2 Bend over the end of the stem into four continuous claw sections, each 1cm (⅜in) in length. Tuck the end of the stem over and through itself to secure the foot shape. Bend a middle section of the stem into an arch, ready to attach to the bird's body. The arch should measure about 2.5cm (1in). Take the remaining length of stem and form the other clawed foot to the same measurements so that they balance correctly. Once both clawed feet are complete, trim away any excess stem, and make sure that the sharp points are buried into the centre of the folds between the four claw sections.

Finishing touches

Sew the eyes to the pompom head with black thread.

Tip   When working the eyes, you might instead like to use a couple of shiny, black beads, but make sure they are large enough to be visible against the bird.

Owl

The fairy landscape would not be complete without the owl to stand guard at night while his fairy and creature friends sleep. The techniques required for this project will by now be quite familiar to you – making lots of different-sized pompoms. The owl is composed of two large pompoms for the head and chest, a medium pompom for the tail section and two small pompoms for the eyes.

Body and head

1 For the body and head, make three large half- and-half coloured pompoms using the cream wool and flecked grey wool. Wind first one colour and then the other around one half each of the pompom discs. Fill the discs completely until there is no room left to fit any more thread through the hole in the middle.

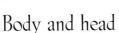

2 For the owl's tail section, create a third handmade pompom using the medium-sized pompom discs.

Equipment and Materials

Pompom discs: Large, 5.5cm (2⅛in) in diameter, medium, 3.5cm (1⅜in)in diameter, and small, 2cm (¾in) in diameter

Sewing needle and thread

Small, sharp pair of scissors

Needle–nose pliers

Sharp pair of utility scissors

50g ball of synthetic, cotton or wool silky grey–flecked thread

50g ball of synthetic, cotton or wool silky white or cream–flecked thread

25g ball of synthetic, cotton or wool orange–flecked thread

2 commercially made pompoms, 5mm (¼in) in diameter (any dark colour)

2 commercially made pompoms, 1cm (⅜in) in diameter (yellow)

1 chenille stem, 30cm (12in) long (any pale colour)

1 pipe cleaner, 10cm (4in) long (beige, brown, black or green)

Actual size 120mm from tip of the tail to top of the head

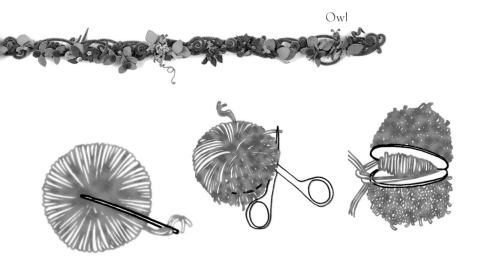

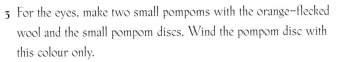

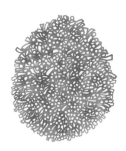

3 For the eyes, make two small pompoms with the orange-flecked wool and the small pompom discs. Wind the pompom disc with this colour only.

4 Taking care that you do not accidentally sever the central thread of the small pompom eyes, clip away the pile from both sides of each, but without altering the diameter and ensuring that you leave a soft, frayed edge to give a feathery effect to the eyes. Your aim is to form two flattish disc shapes which will nestle into the pile of the pompom head without protruding too far beyond the profile of the owl's face.

5 Using the flattish orange pompom eyes as a guideline, trim a little pile away at the top of the forehead to shape a natural outline to the owl's eyes and forehead.

6 Before you join the pompoms together, roll them around to get a sense of their shape. Because they are handmade, the distribution of the pile varies between each, for example one may be more dense than the other and be more appropriate for affixing the pompom eyes, or the coverage of cream wool on one of the pompoms may be more plentiful and therefore better suited to the body of the owl. Use your best judgement to decide which you want to be the head and which the body. Take the three pompoms and line them up in the right order, so that the cream halves are at the front and the grey-flecked halves are at the back. Try to aim for nice streamlined divisions between the front and back colours. Make sure that the pompom tail sits back and at a slight angle under the pompom body, and that the pompom head is embedded nicely into the top of the pompom body and sitting slightly forward from the chest.

7 Using the white or pale-coloured thread and a craft needle, sew the pompom head to the pompom chest, and the pompom tail at the bottom. Pass the needle through all of the pompoms a few times to secure them together. After joining all the pompoms together, weave some thread through the entire length of the body to reinforce the connections and to build up the structure.

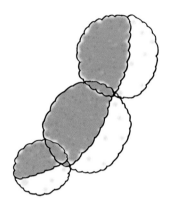

8 If the shape of the tail does not look quite right, trim into shape once it is in position.

9 Place the two flat eye discs and position them onto the head pompom. Leave a white rim that evenly circles the rim of the eyes. Sew these discs firmly into the head pompom shape.

10 To complete the eyes, position the yellow and dark-coloured commercially made pompoms onto the flattish orange pompom eyes so that they are facing inwards in a cross-eyed fashion, and sew into place with the needle and thread.

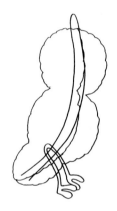

Beak

1 To create the beak, take a pipe cleaner 10cm (4in) long in beige, brown, black or green. Fold over one end of the pipe cleaner, 2cm (¾in) in length. Bend the pipe cleaner over into an arch shape to create the point of the beak, then loop over the other end of the stem.

2 Attach the beak to the pompom head below the two orange pompom eyes.

Clawed feet

1 To create the clawed feet, take a piece of chenille stem 16cm (6⅜in) long in a pale colour, with a knobbly texture. Bend over one end of the stem in a loop to cover the sharp point. Fold the stem into an arch by 2cm (¾in), and then loop into a second claw shape. Wind the remaining length under and loop over to secure the shape. Repeat the same procedure for the other clawed foot. Pinch the middle section into an arch, ready to attach to the body.

2 Position the clawed feet stem around the inner threads connecting the body and tail pompoms. Sew into position using the pale wool thread.

Owl assembly map

This assembly map illustrates all components and stages required to make the owl.

Honey Bea

Honey Bea is a delightful and completely unique creature, part-fairy and part-insect. She is a very satisfying project to make, and uses techniques that will stretch your skills – layering and three-dimensionally weaving Honey Bea's brown tummy stripes, for example, and sculpting the lower and upper parts of the pompom body.

Legs

1 Begin by making the legs out of a 20cm (8in) length of brown or black chenille stem. Bend the stem in half, leaving a curve at the top.

2 Make the bend for the feet about 3cm (1¼in) in at both ends of the stem. Trim away the pile at the ends to form two wedge shapes for the toes.

3 Use the needle-nose pliers to bend them into a curl, then shape the arches and ankles with your sharp scissors.

4 Using the scissors, trim an indentation in the knees just over 3cm (1¼in) from the heel. Clip the backs of both knees into shape, too.

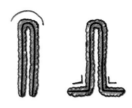

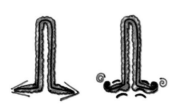

5 With the craft scissors, shape the calf and thigh areas, slightly trimming away the surface of the pile, but be careful not to remove too much material. Bend the knees into position.

6 Once complete, put the legs to one side ready to be attached to the pompom body.

Equipment and Materials

Needle-nose pliers

Sewing needle and thread

Small, sharp pair of scissors

Pompom discs: medium, 3.5cm (1⅜in) in diameter, and small, 2cm (¾in) in diameter

25g ball of wool (bright yellow)

25g ball of wool (brown)

1 pipe cleaner, 30cm x 1cm (12in x ⅜in) (brown or black)

1 chenille stem, 23cm x 5mm (9¼in x ¼in) (brown)

2 commercially made pompoms, 5mm (¼in) in diameter (a dark colour)

2 commercially made pompoms, 5mm–1cm (¼in–⅜in) in diameter

A sheet of 8cm (3¼in) square of opaque plastic

*Actual size: 160mm (6⅓in)
from the tip of the antennae
to the heel*

Arms

1 As a guide, the arms should finally measure about 5cm (2in) long from the top of the shoulder to the hands. Take a 23cm (9⅛in) long brown or black pipe cleaner and cut into four equal lengths to make the arms.

2 For each arm, make a loop in one end with the needle-nose pliers. Twist the loop around a couple of times to create the hand.

3 Using the embroidery scissors, trim away an indentation for the wrist. To shape the inside of the arm, trim away a little of the pile about 1.5cm (⅝in) from the wrist.

4 Make a loop in the other end of the stem for the shoulder, to attach to the body. Refine the arms by shaping the pile with the small pair of scissors, clipping away only a small amount of material at a time.

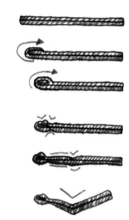

Tail

1 Honey Bea has a stinger tail that sits under the bottom of the pompom body. To make it, take a 5cm (2in) length of the same chenille stem used for the legs. Trim away the pile from one end of the stem to create a gradual wedge-shaped point.

2 Trim away a 2cm (¾in) section of pile from the other end of the stem. Take the trimmed end of the tail piece and wind it around and through the bend in the middle of the legs to secure it.

3 Roll the end into a tight curl with the needle-nose pliers, and position it so that it sticks out at 90° from the legs.

Body and head

1 For the head, make first a small pompom using bright yellow wool and the small-sized pompom disc.

2 For the body, make a second, larger pompom using the medium-sized pompom discs. First wind the entire disc with a couple of evenly distributed layers of yellow wool.

3 Take the brown wool and apply a layer of brown wool on top of the yellow until it is completely covered.

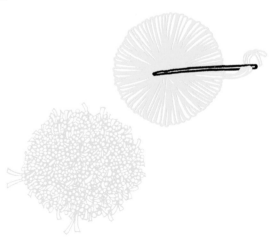

> Tip When winding the wool around the medium-sized pompom disc with alternating layers of colour, make sure the brown stripes fall in the centre of Honey Bea's body. To help you with the right application, select a thin density wool for this purpose. You will not require very much brown wool, so if you have any, make use of leftovers.

4 Wind a further layer of yellow wool until the brown is completely covered, and then another layer of brown. Finally, fill the remainder of the disc with the yellow wool. You will end up with a nicely rounded yellow pompom with two brown strips around the centre.

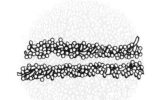

5 Before you assemble the two pompoms, they need to be shaped with the scissors. To create the head, take the small solid yellow pompom and trim away a small area of the surface to form an acorn shape. Adjust the shape as necessary, and tidy up any stray threads of wool. The final head should measure approximately 2cm high by 2.5cm (¾in x 1in) from front to back.

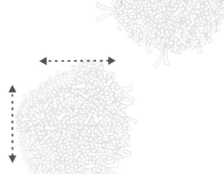

6 To create the upper body shape of the pompom body, remove a significant amount

of pile from the surface. Find the central thread and ensure that it lies on the horizontal. With the small scissors, clip away the thread from the sides of the top yellow section, above the brown stripes. Trim the sides evenly to create a compact middle. You do not need to trim away any pile from the bottom of the pompom; this area should remain untouched. Sew more yellow wool thread into the upper body, and brown into the stripes to build up the density of each.

7 To give the chest area more solidity and definition, weave in additional thread. Without this, it will be difficult for the body to support the weight of the four arms and pompom head.

8 Attach the pompom head to the body and weave additional thread throughout to secure the connection.

9 If you wish, add some form of trim, perhaps of craft felt or lace, between the head and body before sewing into position with a needle and yellow wool.

10 The shape and size of Honey Bea can be adjusted by trimming away with the scissors or threading extra wool into the body. Check its profile and adjust accordingly as you work.

11 Embed the legs into the bottom centre of the pompom body. Using the yellow thread, sew the legs into the pompom body.

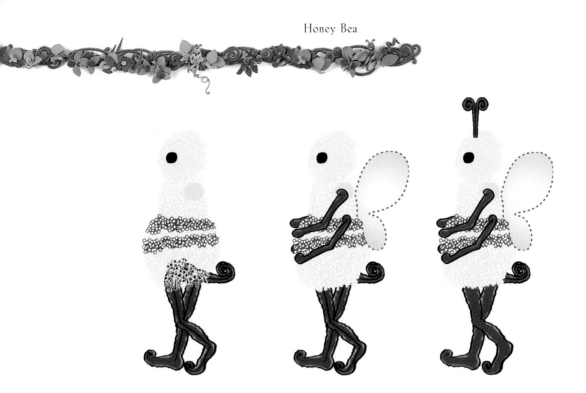

12 Weave additional wool thread throughout the length of the body and the head to reinforce the connections.

13 To make the shoulders, take the two yellow 1cm (⅜in) commercially made pompoms and sew them with fine thread to either side of the chest.

14 Attach the arms to the body with needle and sewing thread. Position one on each side of the shoulder pompoms, and align the two remaining arms at waist level, above the brown stripes.

Wings

1 To make Honey Bea's wings, select the template (see Techniques, page 19).

2 Trace the shape, then cut it out from a piece of transparent or opaque plastic.

3 Perforate the wing with a needle to position the opening for the thread, then attach the wings to the Honey Bea's back with the yellow wool.

Antennae

1 Take a brown pipe cleaner measuring 10cm (4in) long and make a pair of antennae. Begin by trimming the pile down from the length of the stem down to the wire.

2 Using the needle-nose pliers, pinch each end into a curl.

3 Bend the stem in the middle to form a V shape and embed them into the pile at the top centre of Honey Bea's head.

4 Attach the antennae to the top of the pompom head with the yellow wool thread.

Finishing touches

For the eyes, position the two small black commercially made pompoms just below halfway down the pompom head. Space them about 1cm (⅜in) apart at each side of the head. Sew into place.

Honey Bea assembly map

This assembly map illustrates all of the individual components and stages required to make Honey Bea.

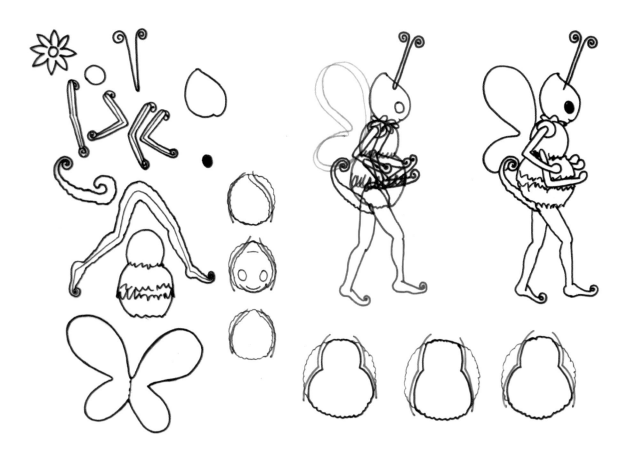

Pink worm

Pink worm is an engaging character with his distinctive bright pink body and yellow breast. Composed of eight handmade pompoms and five commercially made ones, he requires quite a bit of three-dimensional weaving and sculpting with scissors to refine and build up the body.

Body, head and tail

1 To make the head, chest and upper body of the pink worm, make four pompoms using the medium-sized discs. First wind the vibrant pink wool around three-quarters of the disc, then fill the remaining quarter with the bright yellow wool. Wind the wool around the discs until they are full but ensure that each colour is separate. The pink and yellow two-colour pompoms will make up the head, chest and tummy sections of the worm.

Equipment and Materials

Sewing needle

Craft needle

Sewing thread

Small, sharp pair of scissors

Pompom discs: medium, 3.5cm (1⅜in) in diameter, and small, 2cm (¾in) in diameter

50g ball of wool (vibrant pink)

50g ball of wool (bright yellow)

1 commercially made pompom, 1cm (⅜in) in diameter (yellow)

2 commercially made pompoms, 1cm (⅜in) (white)

2 commercially made pompoms, 5mm (¼in) (black or blue)

8 commercially made pompoms, 5mm (¼in) (orange or green)

*Actual size
90mm (3½in) from
the top of the head
to the chest*

Back view

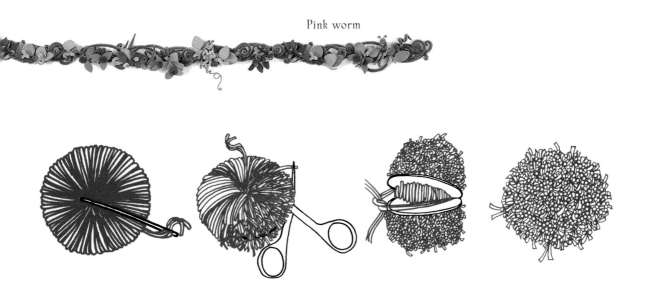

Please note as you work that there will be slight variations in the
sizes of the individual pompoms. If you find that you have one that
ends up slightly larger than the others, set it aside for the head.

2 To make the lower body and tail sections, make four solid pink
pompoms with the small pompom discs.

3 Line up the two-colour pompoms in a row with the yellow
sections facing upwards. Then line the solid pink pompoms in a
row, too, in a slightly offset S shape at the bottom of the two-
colour ones. Each pompom is unique, and some will
have slightly more yellow coverage than others
and may therefore differ in shape.
When positioning the pompoms into
place, try and align the yellow
sections so that they blend into each
other as seamlessly as possible.
Don't worry too much if they do not, as the imperfections add to
the character of the model.

4 Sew all of the pompoms firmly together with the pink wool. Weave
thread throughout the structure of the body to strengthen the
connections and form of the worm. You will find that the top half of
the worm is slightly weightier than the tail end. Keep this in mind
when positioning the curve of the worm's tail so that
the worm is able to balance on it.

5 If you want to build up the yellow sections, weave in additional yellow wool once they are joined together. The extra threads will improve the final density of the character.

6 To create the rounded, bulging eyelids, weave additional pink wool into the pompom head until you achieve the right shapes. They should be positioned on top of the head and slightly forwards. Clip away excess wool to achieve the right shape.

7 Take the small commercially made pompom eyes, position them directly in front of the bulging eyelids and sew securely into place.

8 If you want to adjust and enhance the shape of the worm, build up areas with sewing, and then refine by trimming with the embroidery scissors. This method can be used for any part of this project, more particularly to shape the yellow underbelly, the head, face and eyes of Pink worm.

9 Sew all of the commercially made pompoms into position onto the face. First position one each of the 7mm (¼in) white pompoms to form the white of the eyes, then attach them using white thread. Take the 3mm (⅛in) black or blue pompoms and sew them with a dark-coloured thread on top of the the white ones, positioning them down towards the bottom edge.

10 Using the scissors, sculpt the yellow section of the head into a rounded shape to form the nose and chin area. Cut a groove into the pile to create a smile, and trim along its length on an angle to emphasize and refine the smile.

11 For the nose, position the yellow commercially made pompom directly below the eyes. Sew into place with the yellow sewing thread.

Options

1 If you would prefer to give Pink worm a softer, less refined finish, simply sew all the elements together – and leave the surface untrimmed.

2 If you wish to add detail and highlight the curve of Pink worm's shape, attach tiny orange pompoms onto the centre of each bump, so that they run the length of Pink worm's body. You can vary the positions, as long as they appear to emphasize rather than detract from the curves. Sew these in place with orange thread.

Homes and Hideaways

Curled down under soft, green leaves
Resting wings like cobweb silk
In a hole deep within the trees
A mossy place tight out of sight
Woodland creatures frolic and play
With moonbeams through the night

Leafy lantern

This is a magical little project, and ideal for getting you started on the fairies' homes and hideaways. It is made of craft felt which is a very versatile material and easy to use; it has a soft texture, and is also very strong. It doesn't fray at the edges either, which means that no hemming is required.

Lantern outline

1 Begin by selecting a piece of green craft felt. Make a copy of the template by either photocopying it or tracing it onto another sheet of paper. Overlay the craft felt with the template, and cut around the lantern shape.

2 Score the middle section of the leaf shapes of the lantern outline along the arrow-shaped angles to the point at which the lines end. As you make the incisions, leave the central section of the design as a whole piece so that the leaves remain connected together. Do not cut through this area or the leaves will separate.

Lantern spines

1 Take the two 30cm (12in) green chenille stems and fold over the ends safely. Position them across each other at right angles so that they form a cross. Sew them together where they overlap in the centre.

2 Position the stem cross onto the lantern outline and sew it into place with the green thread. As you sew, be careful to disguise the thread by working it close to the wire of the stem, so that it is hidden in the pile. Use small stitches (shown as red in the diagram, over) and thread through only the surface of the craft felt rather than all the way through. Be as neat as possible.

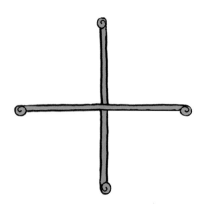

Equipment and Materials

Small pair of craft scissors

Sewing needle and thread (green)

2 chenille stems, 30cm x 5mm
(12in x ⅕in) (green)

1 piece of craft felt, 25cm (9⅘in) square (leaf green)

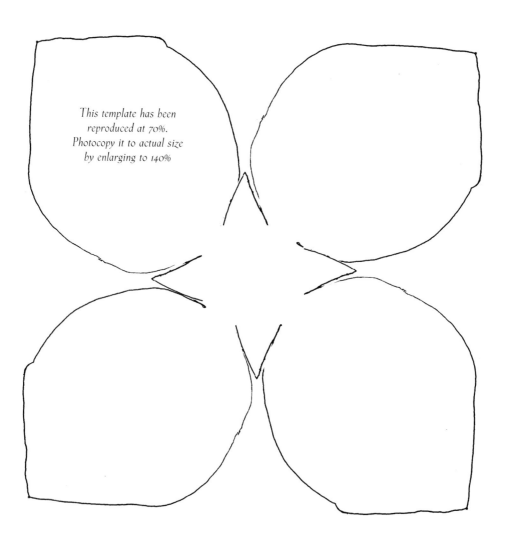

This template has been
reproduced at 70%.
Photocopy it to actual size
by enlarging to 140%

3 Once you have sewn the stems to the felt pattern, gather the sides
of three of the leaf shapes, making sure that the chenille stem
veins are on the outside of the shape. Sew the seams together,
leaving one unsewn to allow an opening in the lantern for the
fairy to be placed inside.

4 The top of the lantern has a solid area of material connecting the
four leaf shapes together. Unravel a small length of stem at the
bottom of the lantern and twist the stems together. The top
section of the chenille stems can be pinched together to create a
pointed shape. Your lantern is now ready to hide away your fairy!

Bird's nest

The bird's nest is a charming home for Baby bird and Blackbird, but is also great for the fairies and creatures to play hide-and-seek! It is made up of about 70 intricately woven pipe cleaners, and is ideal for practising looping, coiling and weaving techniques.

Basic techniques for building a nest

The nest is composed of three main sections – the base, the middle bowl-shaped section and the outer rim. Each section connects via a series of interwoven stems which can be gradually built up into layers to create the structure of the nest.

It is best to make up lots of the different-sized and shaped coils before you begin so that they are immediately to hand. You will find that you build up a more consistent technique if you do so.

1 For the structure of the nest, create a series of long, gently curling stems which are woven together. To make these, hold one end of the stem then pull along the sides of the stems between pinched fingers to create an arch. Alternatively, bend the stem against a cylindrical shape. This is slightly less effective because the stem tends to not remember the shape as well.

2 To make the base of the nest, you need to create a series of large, curling coils. Make one of these by overlapping a chenille stem 23cm (9⅛in) long, through itself to create a loose, pretzel-like knot. To do this, curl over one end of a stem only, then pinch your fingers against the sides of the stem and pull in a circular motion.

Equipment and Materials

Needle-nose pliers

64–70 cotton chenille stems or pipe cleaners,
23cm x 5mm (9⅛in x ¼in)
(natural colours, e.g. moss green, brown, grey,
black or straw yellow)

Tip Develop the structure of the nest gradually, building up the shape by curling, looping and weaving the stems in and out of each other. Don't forget to loop over the ends of the stems to protect your hands against the sharp points. These also add to the knobbly texture of the project.

Top view

Bottom view

*Actual size 116mm
(4⅔in) across*

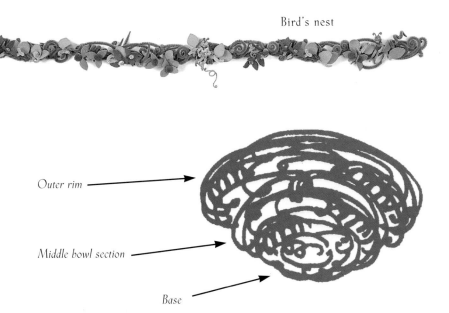

Outer rim ————————

Middle bowl section ————————

Base ————————

Side view of nest

Finish the other end of the stem by folding over the sharp point
with needle-nose pliers.

5 To fill in the gaps in the woven fabric of the nest, make a series of
tight, rounded coils, like a telephone cord. To create these, take an
object, a pencil for example, and wind the stem around it until
curly, pull off and if necessary, push gently into shape. The curls
can also be used to elaborate on the basic nest design, by being
loosely attached to the structure as single curls.

Base

1 Begin by making the base section of the nest. Make one pretzel-
like knot shape as described above. This base coil forms a
foundation to which the other stems can be attached and
then interwoven.

2 Take a second stem and form a loose curl by
gently bending it around a cylindrical object.
Form coils in the length of the stem, flattening
them on top of one another as you work. This
piece attaches to the original coil shape.
Overlap it through the other piece to create a
joined loose open knot shape to form the
bottom of the nest.

Middle bowl section

1 Once the flat base coils are in place, take a looped curved stem and secure it to the sides of the base pieces. To do this, weave one end of the stem only through the base. Pinch it into place with the needle-nose pliers.

2 Take the other, free end of the curved stem and as further stems are attached, weave together to build up the sides of the bird's nest.

3 Continue to attach stems, weaving layers to build up the structure on the inside and outside, until it becomes solid and resembles the shape and size of a small breakfast bowl. The thickness of the walls of the nest will be determined by the density of stems that you interweave.

Outer rim and filling in

1 Use less well-curved stems to create the top outer rim of the nest. Embed these alongside each other to build a kind of outer ledge, and weave them into the fabric of the nest to hold them in place.

2 Finally, make the tight, rounded coils as described above to fill in the gaps in the structure of the nest. The coils are not actually solid pieces, but combined, they make the nest a substantial piece. Again, as you make the coils, position into shape once, then repeat a second time to reinforce the stem's memory.

3 If you like, make other different-shaped stems to place through the coils to secure them into the fabric of the nest. Alter their structure slightly to create a variation in the structure of the weave. If you notice how birds build their nests, the straw or grass often includes a few bent pieces. Leave some stems with loose ends to emphasize the natural appearance of the nest.

Fairy log

The fairy log project is great fun to make, and can be used as both home for the fairies and for hiding away their precious clothes and accessories. The unique character of the fairy log is created by using techniques like wrapping, twisting, weaving and folding the stems to form the knobbly texture and branches. You can vary the size and scope of the project to make your own individual piece.

> **Tip** Have a surplus of pipe cleaners or chenille stems to hand to allow for breakages, or adjustments to the shape and size of the piece.

Building the fairy log

1 To begin making the fairy log, take the cardboard or plastic tube and wind a pipe cleaner around its exterior. Where it overlaps, twist it over and through itself. Attach other looped pipe cleaners to the end protruding from the tube.

2 Tie a further loop-ended stem to the end of the previous one and pinch together. Wind the extended stem around the exterior of the tube and loop it under the other stem to secure it, and out again ready to attach to the next stem. Join all the stems in this way until the tube is covered with a good layer of stems.

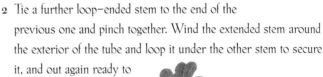

Equipment and Materials

Needle-nose pliers

64 pipe cleaners, each 23cm x 5mm (9⅛in x ¼in) (a natural colour, e.g. moss green)

A cardboard tube, no less than 4–5cm (1½–2in) in diameter

Actual size 140mm (5½in) long

Tip   Remember to use the needle-nose pliers to fold over the ends of the pipe cleaners to protect your skin against the sharp points.

3 To create a branch from the main body of the log, take the end of a stem that has been secured through a loop and begin to twirl the stem around on itself into a coil. Finish the stem off in a coil.

4 Attach another stem to this twisted coil by looping it through, and continue to build up the mass by winding and weaving it until you have a small, intricately curled mound of cotton chenille.

5 To build up more mass in the branches, attach additional stems by looping them into the twisted coil shape and wrap the stem around the outside of the branch. Use the needle-nose pliers to tighten the join between attachments by pinching the looped ends together.

6 You now need to partially remove the tube frame so that the log can be given a naturally twisting profile further along its length. When you have wound about 3cm (1⅛in) of layered pipe cleaners along the tube, begin to ease it away from your original starting point without removing it completely. Remove a little of the tube at a time as you gradually build up the layers of wound and looped stems.

Tip   Vary the size of the fairy log by selecting a larger tube. Ideal containers are cardboard postal rolls, paper kitchen towel rolls or the top parts of good-sized plastic bottles. Avoid using something too narrow or your fairy might get stuck!

7 Using the same method, continue to apply pipe cleaners to the exterior of the tube. Weave these under and over each other, giving the surface of your log a natural-looking, bumpy bark appearance as you work. The log bark can be as thin or as thick as you like by applying more layers of stems through the surface of the material.

8 To add detail, weave twisted and coiled branches into the surface of the bark wherever you like. The branches help balance the base of the fairy log if they are placed at strategic points along the log's length, rather like the feet of a tripod. Continue to build on the log until it reaches approximately 12cm (4¾in) long.

9 When the log is long enough, remove the tube frame altogether.

10 Weave additional pipe cleaners through any patchy areas to give a more solid appearance.

Finishing touches

1 To finish the fairy log, create a door for each end to hide the treasures stored within. Take the needle-nose pliers and create two flat coiled disc shapes, by pinching one end of the stem into a small loop. Hold the loop between finger and thumb and wind the pipe cleaner tightly around on itself until it becomes a coil of the right size.

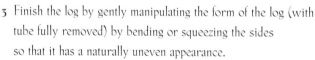

2 Loop the loose end of the disc and attach this to one edge of the log doorways, like a hinge. This enables the door to open and close properly. Repeat this for the second coiled door and attach in the same way at the other end of the fairy log.

3 Finish the log by gently manipulating the form of the log (with tube fully removed) by bending or squeezing the sides so that it has a naturally uneven appearance.

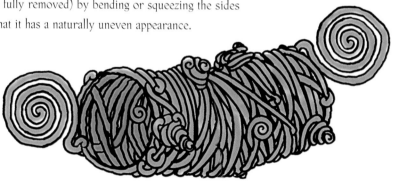

Tip   Use the fairy log to store other fairy and creature objects as well, like fairy slippers and clothes, acorns and bird's eggs.

Bulrush

The bulrush is a fairly complex project, making use of many of the techniques described in this book, but once complete, provides a striking and authentic natural setting for displaying your fairies and creatures.

Stem

1 Start the project by first making the stem of the bulrush. Take three green 30cm (12in) chenille stems and make a loop at one end of each of the three stems.

2 To make the centre of the stem sturdy enough to support the weight of the bulrush head you need to secure the three stems together to form one. To do so, intersect the looped ends of the stems together until secure and pinch to hold firmly. Smooth the stems out with the needle-nose pliers. Keep the rounded ends folded on the inside to protect against sharp points. This rounded end will ultimately project from the top of the head of the bulrush.

3 Reinforce the three-piece stem and maintain its rigid shape by sliding a plastic drinking straw over and around it so that the stems are hidden inside it.

4 Starting at the bottom of the straw, wind a further green stem around its exterior to disguise the plastic straw and give the stem a natural appearance.

Equipment and Materials

Needle-nose pliers

Pompom discs: 2 medium, 3.5cm (1⅜in) in diameter

Sharp pair of scissors

25g ball of wool (brown)

25 chenille stems, 30cm x 5mm (12in x ¼in) (green)

1 plastic drinking straw, 7mm (¼in) in diameter

*View of the bulrush base, showing the
network of woven and looped stems*

*Bulrush shown at half actual size
of 250mm (9¾in)*

Tip You can vary the design of the bulrush stem. For this project I have chosen
to make the stem the same thickness all the way up to the bulrush head, but
alternatively you can make the bottom of the stem thicker than the top by cutting
a section of the plastic straw to reveal the stem within. To do this, cut your plastic
straw into two sections, one 6cm (2⅜in) long and the other 9cm (3⅝in) long. Slide
the first section near to the top of the stem and the second at the bottom, leaving
a visible 6cm (2⅜in) long middle section of green stem. Disguise the bottom
section of straw by winding another green stem around it as before. The
top section of plastic will be hidden by the bulrush head.

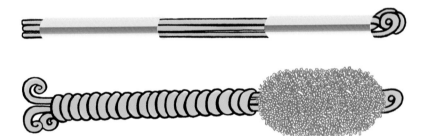

5 To make a base for the bulrush to stand upright, bend the bottom
ends of the three-piece stem outwards into tripod-like feet. With
the needle-nose pliers, bend curls at the very end of each.

Flower head

1 To create the bulrush head, make two identical pompoms using the
medium-sized pompom discs and the brown wool. Wind layers of
thread around the discs until full. Leave enough room in the centre of the disc rings
to be able to fit a drinking straw through them.

2 Slide the bulrush stem through the middle of the first wool-bound pompom disc
until it is in the correct position. Using a pair of sharp scissors, cut through the
threads as normal and separate the discs.

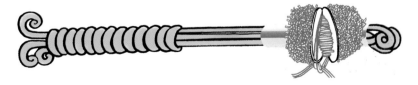

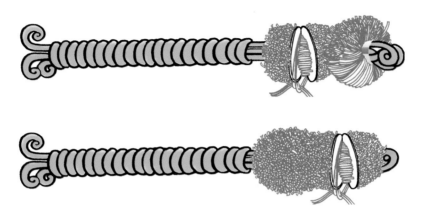

3 With a length of thread, tie the central thread securely to the three-piece stem. Remove the discs carefully. Slide the second wool-bound pompom disc onto the stem, then again cut through the thread and secure it around the central thread with additional wool.

4 Butt the pompoms up close together. Tie the central thread securely around the drinking straw and stem.

5 When both pompoms are attached, make sure that no part of the plastic drinking straw sections are visible through the pompom wool and the wound green chenille stems. If necessary, trim away any excess drinking straw, but be careful not to cut into the chenille pile.

6 Trim away loose threads to refine the edges of the pompoms until they begin to resemble a sausage shape, but again be careful not to clip away too much thread from the top and bottom.

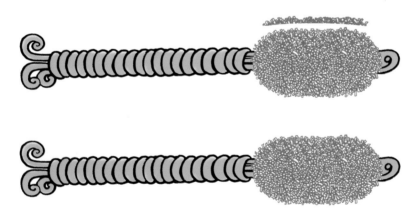

7 To build up the structure of the pompoms to form the bulrush head, first push the pompoms tightly together, then three-dimensionally weave in additional brown thread. Take a craft needle threaded with a double length of wool and pass the needle up and down the length of both pompoms, then criss-cross the needle and thread in the other direction to increase the density of the bulrush throughout until it is perfectly solid.

8 Clip away any stray threads to refine the shape. At this stage, the bulrush flower head pompoms are not secured to the stem, and you may find that it is easier to reach every angle if you can shift it up and down on the stem. Once complete, secure the bulrush head and the stem together, ensuring the drinking straw is completely obscured, by passing the needle and thread through all three elements until the head is firmly in place.

Base

1 Your aim is to build up the structure of the flat base so that the bulrush has enough support, and to create a platform for connecting the chenille stem reeds. First take a green chenille stem and bend it into a circle. Form the circle so that it is just the right size for the curled feet of the three-piece stem to grip comfortably around its edges. Attach the stem base to the circle, pinching the feet securely into place. Avoid looping the ends of the stems before you curl the stem into a circle to protect against scratching your hands as you work. Wait until the circle is formed before looping the ends. Once your circle is complete, you will have a length of excess stem remaining at one end which you will eventually weave into the fabric of the base, but for now leave it as it is.

2 Make a second, larger circle using the whole length of another 30cm (12in) green chenille stem and join the ends together. This piece forms the outer circle of the bulrush base.

3 Place the first, smaller chenille circle with the bulrush stem attached into the middle of the larger, outer circle.

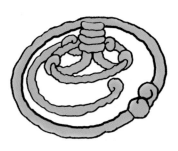

4 You can now begin to build on these two original circles in order to form a grid. Take another green chenille stem and cut it into a 12cm (4¾in) length. This will form one of four chenille petals. Loop one end securely over the outer circle and bend it first into a petal then fold the straight part across the bottom of the outer circle and attach it to the opposite side of the inner circle. The length which crosses the bottom begins to form the grid.

5 Attach a second leaf shape to the outer circle using a 7cm (2¾in) length of the green stem. Any excess stem can be woven back into the centre of the grid and looped through any internal part of the grid.

6 Take another full-length green chenille stem and create another petal shape on the opposite side of the outer circle to the first one. Weave the remaining length of stem back into the grid, passing it through the middle of the circles. Wind it through the centre of the first petal shape and loop onto the outer circle to secure.

7 Weave any excess stem back into the grid and loop through and attach onto another stem.

8 Take a final full-length chenille stem and create the last petal shape to be attached opposite the original one by looping it to the outer circle. Continue to weave the stem through the centre, passing it under and over other stems to build on the base grid. Once folded through to the other side of the circle, wind it around the stem and weave the remaining length through the grid once again.

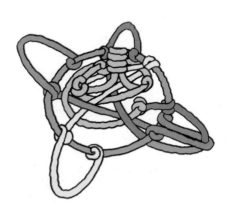

Tip As you work, rather than simply fold the stems under the previous layer, make sure that you weave the stems under and over one another at the base to make the structure stronger.

9 Fill in any gaps with further stems. The bottom should now have a firm structure, ready to attach other stems.

10 Fold over the pointed ends of any stems to protect your fingers when handling.

Reeds

1 Take a full–length green chenille stem and fold it over in half so that you have an arch at the bend. If you like, mould the stem over your finger or a pen to get the right shape. Keeping the stems as straight as possible, loop each end about 1cm (⅜in) apart onto the outer circle to secure into place.

2 Continue to add further stems in the same way to create a bunch of reeds around the edge of the bulrush. Fill the outer circle with the reeds but leave an opening about 2.5cm (1in) wide on one side to allow the fairies room to enter their bulrush hideaway.

3 When attaching the reeds, help to keep them upright by weaving some of the petal shapes through each.

Finishing touches

To finish the base of the bulrush, continue to fill any gaps with stems. Add lengths of chenille stem to the middle of the remaining outside petal shapes to fill them in and make them more solid.

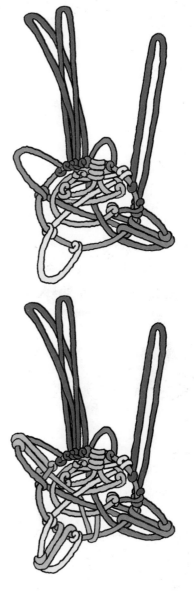

Tip Please note that the colours used to illustrate the base and reeds of the bulrush are not representative of the actual colour of the stems you use. These colours are used to make the processing of inserting stems easier to follow.

Tree house

Like the bulrush, the tree house is a complicated project, but is huge amounts of fun to make, and comes with its own secret compartment for hiding fairies and creatures – the detachable tree canopy! You will need a great many pipe cleaners and chenille stems, but the quantity is flexible depending on the materials you have available and your own design specifications. Once complete, it is surprisingly lightweight.

Tip If you use a cardboard postal tube, it should have a plastic cap at either end to protect the contents. Keep one and put it aside – once the tree house is complete, your characters and other items can be stored inside the centre of the tree trunk.

Tree trunk

1 Begin the project by preparing the cardboard tube to make the tree trunk. I find that any kind of tube will do – from used biscuit containers to the ones you can buy in stationery outlets or post offices. If it helps, measure the length and with a pencil, mark points at 3cm (1⅛in) intervals, then score the cardboard. When you cut through, these marks will help you maintain an even cut. Take a knife or saw to cut the tube to the correct length, approximately 13cm (5⅛in). If you use a saw it is much easier as the cardboard provides very little resistance.

Equipment and Materials

Needle-nose pliers

Approximately 380 cotton-covered pipe cleaners, 23cm x 5mm (9in x ¼in) (brown)

100 chenille stems, 30cm x 5mm (12in x ¼in) (green)

A cardboard tube, approximately 8cm (3⅛in) in diameter

A large bread knife, hacksaw or carpentry saw (for cutting cardboard)

Pen or pencil

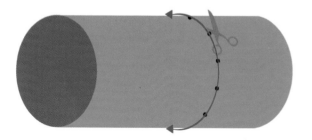

Tree house

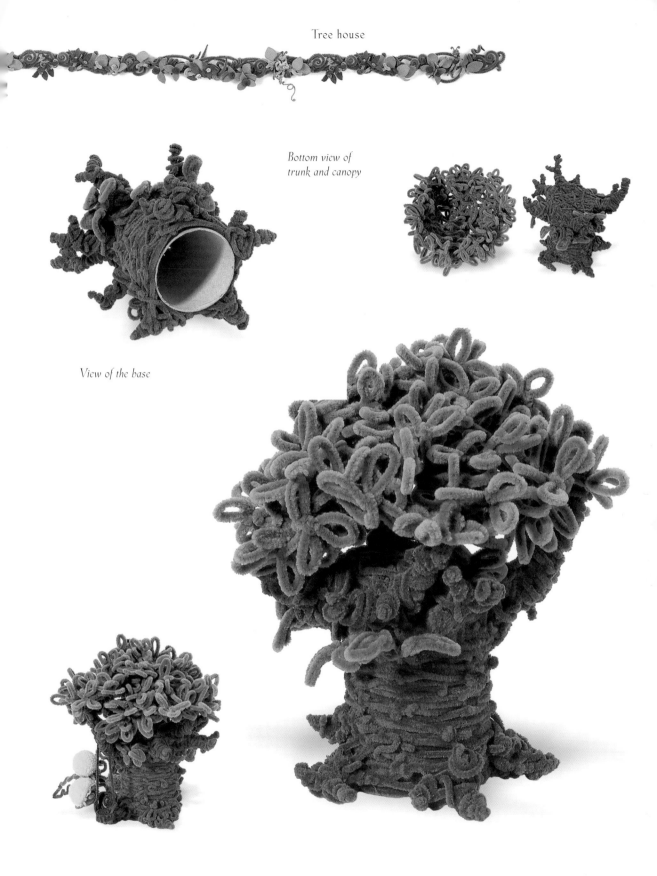

Bottom view of
trunk and canopy

View of the base

2 Now take two brown stems and make a loop at one end of each.
Twist the looped ends of the stems together and pinch with a pair of
pliers to ensure the sharp points are made safe.

3 Wind the joined length of stems horizontally around the uncut bottom
end of the tube. Where the other ends of the stems meet, twist them
together tightly using the needle-nose pliers so that they do not slide
around the tube. Leave any excess stem as it is for the moment.

4 Create a second horizontal band to secure to the top of the tube.

5 Take six further stems to create the vertical
spines through which further stems can be
interwoven to disguise the tube. It is best to
space them evenly apart but is not crucial to the
character of the design. Loop one end of each
vertical stem to the bottom horizontal band and
secure through the top horizontal band. Again,
if your stems protrude beyond the end of the
tube, simply weave these into the fabric of the
tree trunk bark as the project progresses.

6 Wind the loose stem ends of the horizontal
bands back around the tube in opposite
directions, and form loops at the ends.

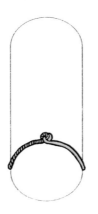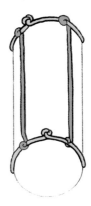

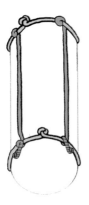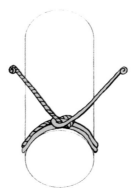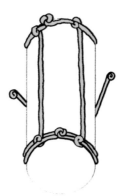

7 Now begin to add layers of further horizontal bands of stems around the tube. Take another brown stem and form a loop at one end. Attach it to the looped end of the original horizontal band, above, and wind it around the tube. Continue the process with further stems, weaving them through the vertical spines and pinching them secure with the needle-nose pliers. As you progress, it will become a little harder to weave through the vertical spines, but the stems should continue to fit through.

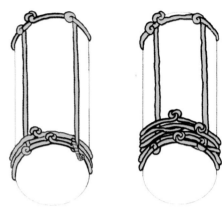

8 Make sure all the stems and connections are tight to the tube so that nothing slips. Fold under all loose points. As you build the layers, the weaving technique will not only make the structure of the tree trunk strong, but produce a natural, bumpy texture to the surface of the bark.

9 Eventually, your tube should be completely disguised, but if you have any bare patches, layer in additional stems, looping over the sharp pointed ends and tying them into existing layers for a thicker surface.

Branches and roots

If you wish, you can add branches, roots, leaves and flowers to your tree trunk, in much the same way as the bark. Attach your branches mainly to the top of the tree trunk to counterbalance the roots at the bottom and to create an appropriately fairytale look.

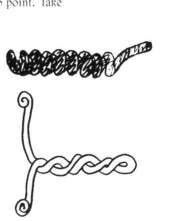

1 To create a branch, begin by making a coil. Take a single brown stem and loop over each end to seal off the sharp point. Take one end of the stem and curl it around a pencil or other, similar item. Hold one end securely against the side of the pencil and wind it around tightly until you have a coil with a fine, tight spring. You can adapt the size of your coil depending on your design.

2 Take another brown stem and fold it in half. Holding the bottom end, use the other hand to twist it like a corkscrew. Leave a little room at the ends of the stems. Form these into loops to protect your hands from the sharp points.

3 Take the twisted, corkscrew stem and insert the coiled stem inside it. You now have a basic branch.

4 Attach the branch by the bottom of the stems to the cardboard tube by twisting and weaving it into the layers of the bark on the tree trunk. Before attaching the top branches of the tree, make sure that the bark is well advanced.

5 To build up the thickness of a branch or root, add further pipe cleaners and wind them into the twisted spine of the branch, or add other coiled stems into the weave of the material. Remember as you work that a branch is wider at its base than its end. Always build up the thickness of the branch after it is attached to the tree trunk. This helps to strengthen the structure and offers more opportunities to enhance the character of the piece.

6 To create a longer branch, join two looped stems together by twisting and then weaving them into a single stem. Fold it over to the desired length but not more than about 10cm (4in) long. If the branch is too long it may become unstable and unravel itself.

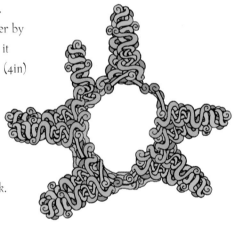

7 Roots are made in the same way as the branches, out of coiled stems, but generally have a more squat shape. When you have made as many as you require, attach the shorter, wider ones to the base of the tree trunk. Arrange them in organic clusters – perhaps two or three together, and balance them with others further around the tree trunk.

Tree branches

8 To add further character and stability to the roots, weave additional stems into them. To maintain strong connections between the roots and the fabric of the tree trunk, make sure you weave, loop and tie the stems tightly. As before, once complete, the texture of the surface of the roots should be bumpy.

Anchor roots

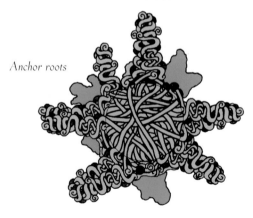

9 Secure the branches at the top of tree trunk by meshing together stems over the opening of the tube, making sure that you tidy the pointed ends by folding them into the grid. This will disguise the hole and create a platform for the leafy canopy.

Canopy

To make the tree's leafy canopy, you need to loop together a series of green leaf-shaped stems to form a hood that fits on top of the tree trunk. It is hollow inside and detachable so that you can lift it on and off as you like to see the characters hidden beneath. The outside edges of the canopy can be elaborated upon to create enough coverage for the branches.

1 Begin by making your first leaf shape. Take a 30cm (12in) long green stem and bend it over a small finger-sized object, a pencil for example, to create a loop. Continue bending the stem to create a second loop immediately next to the first. Bend the stem once more to create a third. Twist them securely together, and pinch the ends to protect against the sharp points.

2 Make sure there is a length of stem left over to which you can attach further looped leaf shapes of the same kind. Joining them in this way is necessary to create the canopy. Once you have completed the first leaf shape, attach it to a single straight chenille stem.

3 Create about 20 looped leaf shapes altogether, following the same method. Attach each leaf shape to the single straight stem by taking one free end of the looped leaf stem and pinching it around it. The straight stem itself acts as a 'mother' stem to which the looped leaf shapes attach. It can be manipulated into a ring, or crown, or left as it is to form a spine linking other sections together. The leaves can be attached to each other in different ways, which evolve as you work.

4 To create the dome-like appearance of the canopy, adjust the leaf shapes so that they are upward-facing, keeping the inside surface of the canopy flat and smooth. Bend and mould the interconnected spines to encourage the dome shape.

Finishing touches

To finish, make a few extra individual leaves and attach them singly to the tree trunk or the roots. This will also help the overall structure. If you want to add any to the top of the tree, create a few which look like leaf buds.

Fairy Furniture

Tiny tail and legs with wings so fast
Up high from a nest full of eggs in hatch
Fallen petals line the way down there
Just looking to sit down softly somewhere

Fairy swing

The fairy swing is a sweet little project, with its stylish wirework design, and provides the fairies with a fun way to relax. You need only five pipe cleaners to make the swing and, once complete, you can elaborate on it to make other furniture for the fairies.

Tip For this project, I recommend using pipe cleaners with a smooth rather than fluffy or knobbly texture.

Seat

1 Begin the project by making the swing seat. Take one of the 23cm (9⅛in) long pipe cleaners and loop over one sharp, pointed end. Hold the looped end firmly between finger and thumb and begin to curl the pipe cleaner around and around until you create a coil. Continue to coil until you have coiled half the pipe cleaner. Turn to the straight end of the stem, and create another coil in the opposite direction. Once complete, you should have a double-ended coil that meets in the middle.

2 Bend the coiled stem at the join between the two so that one coil forms the seat and the other the back. Set this aside for a moment.

Tip To help make the project more straightforward, it is best to make all the individual pieces of the project first, and then join them together.

Equipment and Materials

Needle-nose pliers

5 pipe cleaners, 23cm x 5mm (9⅛in x ¼in)
(moss green or brown)

Fairy swing

Bottom view

*Swing shown at actual size
of 120mm (4¾in)*

3 Next create the rim of the seat. Take a pipe cleaner and pinch the end sections with a pair of needle-nose pliers. Bend the pipe cleaner into a compressed concertina of eleven zigzag folds.

4 Bring the ends together to form a ring and set aside.

5 Take another pipe cleaner to create the sides and the back rest of the chair. This section anchors the seat to the zigzag-shaped bottom rim. Loop over both ends of the pipe cleaner. Using needle-nose pliers, create a pronounced curl at both ends of the pipe cleaner. Fold the pipe cleaner in on itself into a large, oval-shaped loop and knot loosely to secure. Make sure the shape is evenly balanced on either side.

Arms and supports

1 Curve the two side arm loops into a rounded shape following the outline of the bottom zigzag rim. This will be obvious when fitting all of the pieces together.

2 Take another pipe cleaner and loop over the ends of the stem. Fold the stem into an M shape, then bend forward the bottom of the middle section of the M so that it looks like a hook. Make sure the arches in the M shape are curved and not pointed in character.

Swing rope

To create the rope that attaches the swing seat to the branches of the tree house, take a pipe cleaner and loop over each end. Gently curve over the middle of the stem.

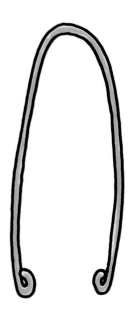

Fairy swing

Assembling the swing

Once you have completed the individual parts, begin to assemble the chair.

1 Take the seat and place it into the centre of the zigzag ring. Make sure the ring grips closely around the seat.

2 Take the back and arm rest sections and place them carefully in position from behind, attaching the sides of each to the zigzag-shaped bottom rim. Be careful to retain the shape of each piece when fitting them together. The back and arm rest sections help to secure the whole thing together.

3 Take the other back support loop and hook section and place the hook in behind the back and through the bottom of the zigzag ring. Using the needle-nose pliers, pinch the bottom hook against the rim to secure the pieces together. Wrap each looped end in through the sides of the chair. Weave these pieces through other sections and attach by pinching them to the sides of the zigzag rim.

4 The last piece to attach to the chair is the swing rope. Take one side of the large loop and weave it down into the side of the chair. Fit it through the arm rest and finish it off by pinching it to the bottom zigzag rim. Follow the same procedure for the other side of the rope loop. Your swing is now complete.

Basket bed

The design for the basket bed is based on traditional willow baskets, and is a delightful project – it's a shame that it is only big enough to fit fairies! It requires very little equipment and materials to make; you need only pipe cleaners and needle-nose pliers.

Base

1 Begin the basket bed by creating the base section. First take three pipe cleaners and bend loops at the end of each then join them to one another, end to end.

2 Pinch down on both sides of each loop with the needle-nose pliers to seal the joins. Work with the pipe cleaners as though it is one long stem.

3 Holding one end firmly between finger and thumb, rotate the length of pipe cleaners in your hand, keeping the stems close together to form a tightly rounded disc. The final diameter of the disc should be approximately 6cm (2⅜in). When you let go of the disc, it might unravel slightly.

4 Next cut two 8cm (4⅜in) lengths of pipe cleaner to form crossbars for the bottom of the basket bed. Take one and weave it over and under the spirals across the centre of the disc. Be careful to keep the stems as straight as possible. If you like, use the needle-nose pliers. Take the second stem and repeat, weaving it through the spirals of the disc in the other direction, to form a cross.

5 Once woven through, leave about 1cm (⅜in) of the end of each stem protruding beyond the outer edge of the spiral disc shape. These four short sections form useful tabs which you can use to join the base to the outer walls of the basket bed.

Equipment and Materials

Needle-nose pliers

Utility scissors

27–30 cotton-covered pipe cleaners, 23cm (9⅛in) long (any colour)

Basket bed

*Actual size 70mm (2¾in)
from the base to top of
the hood*

Side view

Bottom view

Outer walls

1 Connect nine pipe cleaners by looping them together at the ends as before to create a long length of pipe cleaners. Pinch the ends with the needle-nose pliers to seal the bond.

2 Bend the stems into even concertina folds, each 3cm (1¼in) long, until you have completed the length of the stem. This shape has the flexibility to allow either the top or base to expand and splay outwards into a curve.

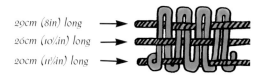

29cm (8in) long →
26cm (10¼in) long →
20cm (11¾in) long →

3 Take three further stems and weave evenly spaced horizontal spines through the vertical concertina folds to build up the structure. To get the correct lengths, cut the one nearest the base to a length of 20cm (8in), the middle one to a length of 26cm (10¼in), and the top one to a length of 29cm (11¾in). To achieve the longer lengths, loop a shorter length of stem onto another longer one. Once your weaving is complete, the loops will not show in the fabric of the bed, and at any rate, add character. Leave a bit of overlapping stem on both of the three spine pieces to use to attach the sides together.

4 Attach the sides together to form the basket shape.

Assembling the base and outer walls

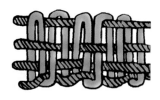

1 Attach the basket base you have made to the narrower end of the outer wall section. Take a stem and bind the two together by weaving through the outside edge of the base and the bottom spines of the outer wall section.

2 Loop the tabs protruding from the the base up through the chenille fabric of the sides of the basket bed. The top part of the outer walls should be wider than the bottom, but if you find this is not the case, adjust by gently easing them further apart at the top.

3 Remember to pinch the sharp ends together to make them safe.

Hood

1 To make the hood for the basket bed, begin by joining ten whole pipe cleaners, end to end, to form one continuous length.

2 Fold the length into concertina folds that measure 4cm (1½in) on each side, rising gradually to 6cm (2⅜in) in the centre. Do not worry about bending the stems in exact increments; the important consideration is to make the shape a nice, even curve and to make at least three of the centre concertina folds the longer length. This concertina shape should ultimately measure about 10cm (4in) in length, and will look different from that of the outer walls because it curves on one side and is straight on the other.

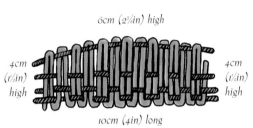

6cm (2⅜in) high

4cm (1½in) high

4cm (1½in) high

10cm (4in) long

3 For the horizontal spines, take four further whole pipe cleaners and using the needle-nose pliers if necessary, weave them through the concertina folds as shown. Be careful to maintain a straight line as you weave.

4 Trim off the protruding ends, leaving about a 1cm (⅜in) tab which you can use to secure this section to other parts.

5 Once your basket hood is woven, begin to bend the hood into shape by pressing it into the cup of your hand. Alternatively, use a round object like a spoon to ease it into shape. It is now ready to fit onto the walls of your basket.

6 To attach the hood to the top of the basket, weave a stem through both the hood and the outer walls as though you are oversewing them together. Leave a gap at each side of the hood/wall join about 3cm (1½in) wide to allow two further curled disc shapes to be inserted.

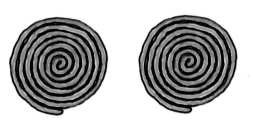

7 Make the discs using a whole pipe cleaner for each and following the same method as before. Loop the end of each disc and use it to weave into the basket hood and secure into position.

8 Finally, weave a stem through the top spines of the basket rim to seal off any open edges and secure all the pieces together.

Treasure Trunk

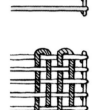

The treasure trunk is a magical little project — perhaps one of the fairies found it at the bottom of the sea and has brought back to delight her friends.

   The project is a little more challenging than some of the others — the complexity lies in ensuring that the pipe cleaners for the walls of the trunk remain equally spaced, and this increases as the grid expands in size. It just requires a little care and patience. You will find the size of the design used here quite manageable, but if you like, you can make the trunk larger by adding further pipe cleaners to build up the grid.

Front and side panels

1 To begin this project, you first need to make up the front and back panels for the trunk. Take seven whole pipe cleaners, making sure that they are perfectly straight. Loop over the end of each. Attach them at even intervals to another 5cm (2in) section of pipe cleaner, rather like a flag on a mast. Take a second 5cm (2in) section of pipe cleaner and loop the other ends of the pipe cleaners to it so that it is firmly attached. You now have a rectangle through which to weave a grid.

2 Now cut 18 stems to 9cm (3½in) in length. Take the first pipe cleaner and, starting about 1cm (⅜in) away from the mast-like pipe cleaner at one end, begin to weave it vertically through one of the outside edges of the horizontal row of pipe cleaners.

3 Weave it through the seven long horizontal pipe cleaners and leave a short tab protruding beyond the end. This acts as an anchor to attach pieces together further on in the project. When you have woven it to the end of the row, bend it over and weave it back the way it came. The returning length of pipe cleaner should be spaced about 1cm (⅜in) apart from its outgoing length. Make sure the folded-over section is secured around the outer horizontal pipe cleaner in an even curve.

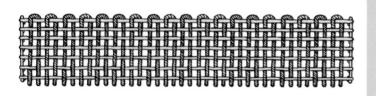

Equipment and Materials

Needle-nose pliers

Utility scissors

36 cotton-covered pipe cleaners, 23cm (9½in) long (any colour)

132

Treasure trunk

Side view

Actual size 70mm (2¾in) across base

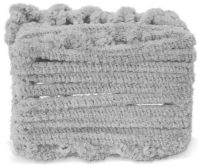

Bottom view

4 Continue to weave the remaining pipe cleaners through the seven horizontal ones until you form a pattern like a grid. Use the needle-nose pliers to keep them in straight lines. The number of pipe cleaners you require to complete this may vary depending on how closely you space them together as you weave. The idea is to fill the seven horizontal pipe cleaners until the rectangular grid is full. The tighter the weave, the more substantial the sides of the trunk will be.

5 You will now have many protruding ends at the bottom outer edge of the grid. For the moment, loop them over to make them safe; they can be straightened again and pinched down when you are ready to use them to attach the grid to other pieces of the trunk. You now have a flat, rectangular grid, ready to manipulate into a trunk-like shape.

6 Holding the grid widthways in front of you, first establish the centre point of the grid and measure 3cm (1¼in) in either direction. These dimensions will form the 6cm (2⅜in) parameters of the front section of the trunk. Bend the grid against the corner of a table or box to form a sharp right angle to create this front panel.

7 To establish the side sections, measure 4cm (1⅝in) from the edges of the front panel and fold back both side sections to create a partial box shape.

8 Once folded, the edges of the walls should meet in the middle to close the box shape. The seam edges overlap each other slightly at the back of the trunk to allow some flexibility when fitting and adjusting the attachment around the top edges. Set this section of the trunk aside for a moment.

Lid

1 To create the lid of the trunk, cut six pipe cleaners to 13cm (5⅛in) long. These lengths form the grid that runs the width of the lid of the trunk.

2 Take one of these and bend it in half over either a knitting needle, thin pencil or paintbrush stem to give it a nice curve. Make sure the ends meet up evenly. Bend the remaining five pipe cleaners in the same way.

3 Loop one end of each, and place all six lengths, looped ends together, in a row on a flat surface about 1cm (⅜in) apart.

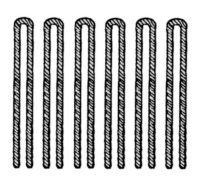

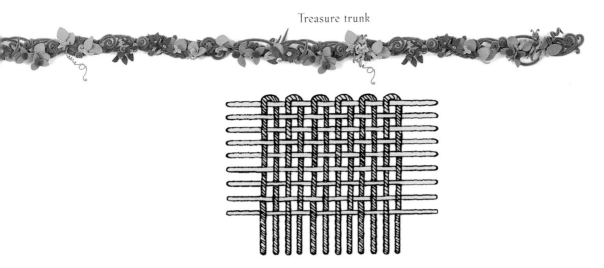

4 Cut nine further stems 11cm (4¼in) in length. Begin to weave them through the six folded-in-half lengths of pipe cleaner. As you work, make sure they are straight and spaced about 1cm (⅜in) apart. Once woven, you should have protruding ends, or tabs, measuring about 2cm (¾in) long at each end. Try to ensure that they are even in length, but if they are not, any shortfall will blend in. Bend these over at 1cm (⅜in) to form the lip of the trunk lid.

5 Take three additional stems and weave them through the length of the tabs, all the way round the grid that forms the lip of the lid. Use the needle-nose pliers to keep them in a straight line. Pinch everything together so that it is neat and secure. Secure the sharp ends by pinching them into the grid of the lid to seal them off after the longer stems have been woven through the lip. You now have the complete lip to the lid of the trunk, with an opening at the back of the lid to secure to the trunk.

6 Attach the lid to the back of the trunk by taking another stem and manipulating it as though oversewing, through the lid and the back wall of the trunk. The lid should be slightly larger than the body of the trunk so that the sides of the lid grip comfortably around the walls of the trunk. If necessary, the size of the walls can be altered by pinching the back seam closer together or, if necessary, by adding additional material to the weave. Seal the connection in the back of the box by looping together with a small length of leftover pipe cleaner. Pinch these connections with the needle-nose pliers.

Base

1 To create the base of the trunk, cut ten straight stems to a length of 7.5cm (3in). Make a loop at the end of each of the pipe cleaners.

2 Take the trunk as it stands, and attach the first pipe cleaner by looping it through one of the narrow edges of the open bottom of the body of the trunk. Take the same pipe cleaner and loop the other end through the other side, to complete the connection. Pinch it down to secure.

3 Take a second stem and insert it next to the
   first and repeat the process. Fill in the
   entire base of the trunk with the remaining
   pipe cleaners, until you have a solid
   bottom. Your completed treasure trunk
   should finally measure just over 6cm (2⅜in)
   in width, 5cm (2in) in height and 4cm (1½in)
   deep from front to back.

Hooks and latches

1 To make the hooks and the latches for the trunk,
   you need only one full-length stem. Using the
   needle-nose pliers, fold to create the individual
   shapes, as shown, right.

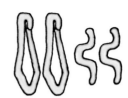

2 Before you attach them, play with the position of
   both the hooks and the latches to make sure that
   they fit comfortably. Attach the hooks to the
   front of the grid, on the outside of the middle
   of the trunk, by inserting the ends through
   the weave and pinching them into the wall of
   the trunk on the inside to secure them. If it
   is helpful, use the needle-nose pliers.

3 To attach the latches, slip the thin ends of
   the hooks in through the front edge of the
   top of the lid. Twist them around and pinch
   them into the weave of the trunk lid. Once
   closed, they should fit together cleanly.

Final touches

1 To add detail to the trunk, take a full-length pipe cleaner and wrap it firmly around
   the outside of the trunk, slightly above the base. Once it has gone all the way
   around, secure it tightly by twisting it into a knot. Use the needle-nose pliers if
   necessary. If you have any extraneous pipe cleaner, fit it neatly through the mesh to
   disguise it.

2 Using a kind of blanket stitch, weave a pipe cleaner through the edge of the top rim
   of the walls of the trunk. Weave another to the edge of the base of the trunk at both
   the front and the back.

Fairy Flowers and Creature Comforts

Acorns polished to a copper glow
Hidden safely in hedgerows
Gather all enough to last
Summer's send off, bounty made
Honeycombs and daisy chains
Winter's on its way again

Berry

The berry is a very appealing project, and children especially love it for its colour and pocket-sized shape. It is a great project to help you polish your three-dimensional weaving and colour-blending skills and, as it requires only a little shaping and carving with a small sharp pair of scissors, is ideal for getting you started on the fairy and creature comforts.

Berry

1 To begin the berry, make a medium-sized pompom. Take the 3.5cm (1⅜in) pompom discs and wind the berry red wool around them. Fill in this colour three-quarters of the way round the discs, and wind the remainder with the bright green wool until it is so absolutely full, a needle cannot pass through the middle.

2 Cut the wool from the centre of the discs and tie the central thread with the berry red wool.

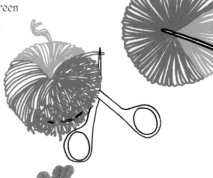

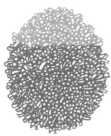

Tip   If you wish, add accent colours to the berry red wool. For a more natural appearance, add a darker red wool to the mix, and for detail, intersperse litte dots of pale yellow to emulate seeds. Use the same-textured wool for consistency.

Equipment and Materials

Sewing needle

Small pair of sharp scissors

Pompom discs: medium, 3.5cm (1⅜in) in diameter

25g ball of wool (berry red)

25g ball of wool (dark red red)

25g ball of wool (bright green)

Craft felt, 14cm (5½in) square (bright green)

Berry

Actual size 50mm (2in) across

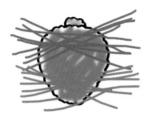

3 Use the craft scissors to trim pile away from the sides of the pompom berry to give it a gently pointed bottom end.

4 Remove pile from the green top part of the pompom to create a small bump in the centre. Continue to shape the end point at the bottom by removing material from the sides.

5 At the same time as you remove excess threads, weave additional thread into the centre of the pompom to develop a more solid structure, and this will also refine the outline of the berry. Weaving extra wool through the berry gives more solidity to the structure of the fruit and better definition, for a more realistic result.

Final touches

Add a green craft-felt trim to the centre of the green bump at the top of the berry and attach by sewing firmly to the centre.

Trim pattern

Pretty pink flowers

These pretty little flowers are a joy to make and extremely useful as a decorative accessory for all kinds of fairy or creature settings. For this project I have chosen pink chenille stems to make the flower petals, but you can vary the colour according to your design.

Tip   When selecting colours for your pipe cleaners, choose those colours in the same 'family', such as orange or red, and the same material and pile texture. This means that your flowers will look natural and blend harmoniously together.

Flowers

1   Begin the project by assembling a quantity of the long pink chenille stems. To create the flower shapes, take one of the pipe cleaners and loop over one of the ends into a hook to join the other end of the pipe cleaner once it is formed into a flower head.

2   Fold the pipe cleaner 1.75cm (⅜in) along the straight end of the stem. This length will form both the join to be secured into the hook, and the stalk of the flower head.

3   Fold six petal–shaped loops into the length of pink chenille stem, each one about 3cm (1⅛in) in length. To help you form nicely rounded loops for the petals, fold the stem around the tapered end of a pen or other similar object.

4   Hook the original straight length into the hook to secure the flower head shape and use the needle–nose pliers to pinch together the connection.

Equipment and Materials

Craft scissors

Needle–nose pliers

Sewing needles and thread

2–12 cotton chenille stems, 14cm (5½in) long (pink)

2–12 chenille stems, 30cm x 5mm (12in x ¼in) (green)

2–12 commercially made pompoms, 5mm (¼in) in diameter (bright yellow or orange)

Actual size 120mm (4¾in) wide

Back view

5   To give the petals a naturally unfolding shape, use the needle-
    nose pliers first to pinch the join in the centre, and then to
    manipulate them to adjust the shape.

6   Once you have shaped your flower, make the mass of stamens
    by placing a 5mm (¼in) – or larger, if you wish – commercially
    made pompom in the middle of the petals. Using a needle and
    thread, secure all the elements firmly together – chenille stem
    petals and pompom – by sewing them in place.

Greenery

1   To create the green stalks and leafy section, take a long, green chenille stem and
    taper the ends by trimming with a pair of scissors, in the same way as you have to
    sculpt feet for the fairies.

2   Take the needle-nose pliers and curl the ends of the stem. By doing so, you cover
    the sharp end of the wire, and give the greenery a natural, organic appearance.

3   Once complete, take the green stem and begin to wind it around the stalk of the
    pink pipe cleaner approximately 2cm (¾in) from the tapered end, to
    form a tendril. Then continue to wind the remainder of the stem
    around the pipe cleaner stalk, so that it looks like a twist.

4   Make a second flower following the same procedure. Trim
    and wind the other end of the same green chenille stem
    around the stalk of this flower so that they join at the bottom.
    This connecting stem acts as a bridge that can be used to
    attach other flowers, to form a mass of flower clusters with
    a profusion of greenery at their base. Bend and twist
    these bridges together and use these sections as the
    basis for a flowerbed. You can add on more
    flowers, stalks and greenery to extend your
    flowerbed as much as you like.

Lily pad and flower

The lily pad and flower is a delightful accessory for the fairies and creatures, and the design can also be adapted to make other leaves and flowers, like a rose, daisy or dandelion. Once you have made one, the possibilities are endless. This is another great starter project, and enables you to make use of your pompom-making skills as well as pattern-cutting and sewing. If you have a sewing machine, all the better – you can use it to join the lily pad leaves together, and to decorate the pad with zigzag veins.

Lily pad

1　To begin the lily pad, take a piece of green craft felt, and using the template provided (see page 146), cut out two lily pad leaves.

2　The lily pad is composed of two layers of felt, one on top of the other. Sew the edges together with blanket stitch, which lends the lily pad a natural, rippled edge.

3　To transfer the veins to the pieces of felt, trace the design illustrated on the template onto a piece of paper. Cut out the shape from the paper and place it into the centre of the fabric. Using a felt-tip pen in a darker green, apply the design to the fabric.

4　Next, use either your needle and sewing thread, or put the felt pieces on the sewing machine and apply a zigzag stitch to oversew the felt-tip veins.

Equipment and Materials

Sewing needle

Small, sharp pair of scissors

Craft scissors

Pompom discs: medium, 3.5cm (1⅜in) in diameter

Craft felt, 17cm (6¾in) square (green)

Craft felt (pale pink)

Craft felt (pale yellow)

25g ball of wool (green, to match the craft felt)

25g ball of wool (deep yellow)

Water-based felt-tip pen (dark green)

Embroidery thread (dark green) (optional)

Lily pad and flower

Shown half actual size

This template has been reproduced at 70%. For the actual size, photocopy at 140% or use the A4 to A3 setting

Lily flower

1 To create the lily flower, begin by making a pompom using the medium-sized pompom disc. First, wind two-thirds of the disc with the yellow wool, then follow this with the green wool, filling the remaining one-third of the disc until the centre hole is packed with wool.

2 Using a small, sharp pair of scissors, cut down the centre of the pompom, severing the thread to separate the discs.

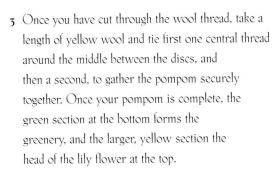

3 Once you have cut through the wool thread, take a length of yellow wool and tie first one central thread around the middle between the discs, and then a second, to gather the pompom securely together. Once your pompom is complete, the green section at the bottom forms the greenery, and the larger, yellow section the head of the lily flower at the top.

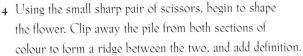

4 Using the small sharp pair of scissors, begin to shape the flower. Clip away the pile from both sections of colour to form a ridge between the two, and add definition.

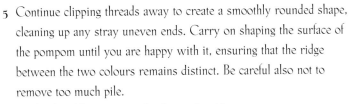

5 Continue clipping threads away to create a smoothly rounded shape, cleaning up any stray uneven ends. Carry on shaping the surface of the pompom until you are happy with it, ensuring that the ridge between the two colours remains distinct. Be careful also not to remove too much pile.

6 To finish, add stamens to the flower head by sewing several separate double-thicknesses of thread into the centre of the pompom fabric. Tie a knot in each of the stamens, about 1.5cm (⅝in) up, and cut away the remaining thread above it.

Petals

1 To make the petals, use the templates provided first to trace and then use them as a guide for cutting out the shapes from the pink and yellow craft felt. You will need eight petals of each colour, in different sizes, small and large.

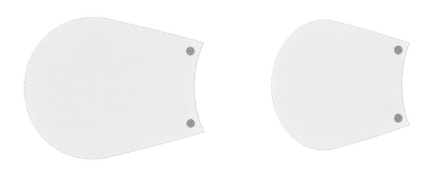

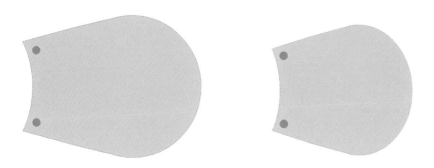

2 Before you attach the petals, think about how you want to arrange them around the flower head. First sew the large pink petals at the very bottom, then the large yellow ones on top, the small pink petals on top of those, and finish with a layer of small yellow petals on the very top. For a natural look, as you attach them with yellow wool to the central ridge of the pompom, pinch together each one towards the centre to form a dart. Ensure also that they overlap slightly and do not obscure each other.

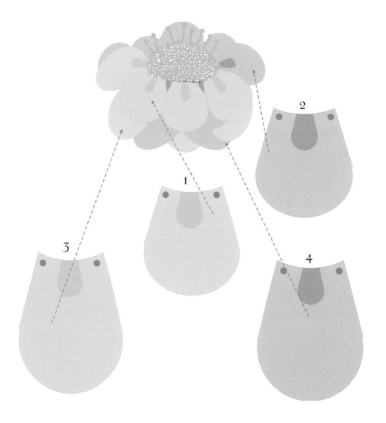

Toadstool

The toadstool is very appealing, with its quirky, organic shape – and is perfect for seating all sizes and shapes of fairies and creatures. It is a good medium-level project which makes good use of your three-dimensional weaving skills, and includes a unique method for stabilizing the structure of the stalk.

Cap

1 To begin the project, start by making a pompom for the cap of the toadstool. Take the large-sized pompom discs and wind them two-thirds of the way round with beige wool. Wind a second wool in a darker shade of brown around the final third of the cap. The darker brown represents the underside of the cap.

2 Now make two smaller beige pompoms using the small pompom discs.

3 Trim away any excess wool from the surface of all three pompoms to refine them.

4 Find the central thread to establish that each pompom is horizontal. This will be more apparent on the larger pompom because the bottom section has the darker brown wool.

5 Take the large pompom and trim pile away from the dark bottom section, then begin to round out the cap.

6 Continue to shape the outer edges and thread additional beige wool through the toadstool cap to develop a rim on the edge of the colour break. The rim should be about 1cm (⅜in) in depth.

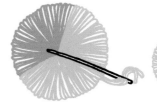

Equipment and Materials

Sewing needle

Small pair of sharp scissors

Needle-nose pliers

Pompom discs: Large, 5.5cm (2⅛in) in diameter; small, 2cm (¾in) in diameter

25g ball of wool (beige)

25g ball of wool (brown)

Pipe cleaner or chenille stem, 23cm (9⅛in) long

*Shown actual size 90mm (3½in) from
top of the cap to base of the stalk*

Bottom view

7 Clip away dark thread from the bottom of the cap to flatten the surface. Once complete, this section will not be terribly visible, but the break in colour is important for defining the shape and character of the toadstool. The stalk of the toadstool will be positioned into the underside of the cap.

Stalk

1 Position the two small pompoms together and clip away some of the surface before sewing them together to form a sausage shape.

2 Clip pile away from the sides of the stalk to refine it.

3 Trim away some pile from the top and bottom of the pompom stalk. The bottom of the stalk should have a slightly rounder character than the top, but should remain stable when upright.

Assembling the toadstool

1 Attach the cap and stalk together by sewing thread through the centre and weaving in additional thread. This builds up the structure and makes the core of the toadstool more solid.

2 Once the structure is complete, take a knitting needle or other similar object, and push this into the centre of the stalk and cap to create a hole right through. This cavity needs to be large enough to allow a single 23cm (9⅛in) long pipe cleaner to pass through.

3 When the stem breaks through the top of the cap, fold and curl over the end to create a knot or loop.

4 Pull the stem back into the body of the toadstool, to lodge just beneath the surface of the cap. The remainder of the pipe cleaner should be visible at the bottom of the toadstool. Take this and fold it into three loops to create a flat support at the bottom of the stalk.

5 Wind these loops with the wool to disguise the base and sew it into the pile to secure it. Your toadstool now has a spine which will allow the toadstool to stand alone.

Index

About The author

Julie Sharp trained in Canada. An illustrator, her passion is for working in 3D, and her work includes commissions for the advertising and publishing fields.

Influenced by her own childhood interests, in the early 1990s she was inspired to develop new weaving and sculpting techniques to create unique characters which appeal to children and adults alike, and reflects her personal belief in using art to develop creativity in others.

She lives with her family in London.

Createchures.com